HOW TO
RAISE KiDS
WITH INTEGRITY

A Guide for Parents, Childcare Educators & Teachers

I0088544

GLOBAL
PUBLISHING
G R O U P

Global Publishing Group
Australia • New Zealand • Singapore • America • London

HOW TO
RAISE KiDS
WITH INTEGRITY

A Guide for Parents, Childcare Educators & Teachers

Trish Corbett

DISCLAIMER

All the information, techniques, skills and concepts contained within this publication are of the nature of general comment only and are not in any way recommended as individual advice. The intent is to offer a variety of information to provide a wider range of choices now and in the future, recognising that we all have widely diverse circumstances and viewpoints. Should any reader choose to make use of the information contained herein, this is their decision, and the contributors (and their companies), authors and publishers do not assume any responsibilities whatsoever under any condition or circumstances. It is recommended that the reader obtain their own independent advice.

National Library of Australia
Cataloguing-in-Publication entry:

Trish Corbett
How to Raise Kids with Integrity
A guide for parents, childcare educators and teachers

1st ed.
ISBN: 9781925288759 (pbk.)

A catalogue record for this
book is available from the
NATIONAL
LIBRARY
OF AUSTRALIA
National Library of Australia

Published by Global Publishing Group
PO Box 517 Mt Evelyn, Victoria 3796 Australia
Email Info@GlobalPublishingGroup.com.au

For further information about orders:
Phone: +61 3 9739 4686 or Fax +61 3 8648 6871

For Matt, Danica, Maison & Ivy
You are the reason I want the
world to be a better place
You are my world

ACKNOWLEDGEMENTS

Lisa of Zen Word Whisperer Book Editing

Special thanks to Lisa, who has been an absolute pleasure to work with and has been so supportive throughout this journey I have undertaken, even though we are on opposite sides of the world. Lisa Petr, you are a wonderful amazing woman, who I one day hope to meet in person! Thank you for being so flexible, committed, loyal and reliable by collaborating with me in order for this book to make it out there into the world – and a special thanks for making me sound so much better than I am!

Helen Rankin & Nadja Cregan

Helen – Thank you for introducing me to Lisa. It was a blessing meeting you that day. Everything happens for a reason as they say! So very grateful that you have an open heart and were willing to share your knowledge, and editor with me. Thank you from the bottom of my heart.

Nadja – I have enormous gratitude for you for providing the excellent service of proofreading this book once written – I truly appreciated your invaluable input and efficiency.

Global Publishing Group

Darren, Jackie, Helen, Kelly and Darlene, thank you for the inspiration, encouragement and excellence of service, shown by doing what you do so well. Words are not enough to express my gratitude for the faith you placed in me to write this book, as well as the tolerance and call for self-discipline, when I needed it. Thank you.

Linda Kavelin-Popov

Endless respect, gratitude and so much more goes to Linda Kavelin-Popov, co-founder of The Virtues Project™ along with her amazing husband Dan Popov and brother John Kavelin (your memory lives on). Linda is the example and role model that I aspire to be. The Virtues Project™ was the seed from which this book grew, as it was the first self-development course I attended and I am so deeply passionate about, as it taught me the power of positive language.

To my family – My parents, Margaret & Trevor, my siblings, Angela, Margaret, Danny & Brian, and their families. Every day I am grateful for being a part of this wonderful close family, physically and emotionally and to my wonderful sister-in-law, who likes to tell people, we even like each other! Thank you for always being there for me – I love you all so much! Plus my extended family – loving aunts, kind uncles and amazing cousins.

To my friends – I am blessed to have so many incredible, loving, generous friends gifted to me by the universe, as they have assisted me throughout this journey and by motivating me when I needed it. Thank you for your constant support and highly valued friendship – Jenni Cook, Jo & Mal Sheens (you guys are the epitome of this book), Lizzy Johnson, Joelle Harding and Phil Lloyd, Jacky Barlow, Arky James, Kate Maul, Marita Rifai, Ruth Cardier, Farrokh Fanaiyan, Neda & Marzi, the Currie family (my other family), Bruce & Tracey Painter, Leonie Rothman (how awesome are you!!), Christine Yee, Sophie Sharman, Michelle Myint plus so many other wonderfully supportive and inspirational people. My sincere apologies if I've neglected to mention anyone who has supported me through this amazing journey. Thank you.

To you – I have met many other extraordinary people, having attended numerous personal and professional development courses, and they all, like you, make a difference in their own special way as they strive to make the world a better place – thank you to everyone who fits this bill – you make the world a better place! Thank you reader for wanting to make a positive difference in this world.

BONUS OFFER

FREE 30 Minute Discovery Session

As my gift to you, spend 30 minutes with me
personally, and in that 30 minutes we can talk about
you and aspects of your life that are important to you,
and within that 30 minutes I will guarantee you that
you'll know what your next step needs to be.

You can contact me via my website –
www.ethicalfoundations.com.au

If you've ever wondered about what life coaching is
about then take the opportunity to spend 30 minutes
with me.

TABLE OF CONTENTS

DISCLAIMER

I'm not a perfect parent, role model or coach, but really, who is in life? I believe that we all try to do the best we can as parents, childcare educators and teachers, but we can all use some help on our journey, to becoming supportive and compassionate role models. This is why I created the nine Personal Awareness Components (9-PAC) Integrity Approach Model.

I am not a doctor, psychologist, therapist, naturopath, counsellor or a medical practitioner of any type. This book is not to be used in place of medical treatments or medical advice. My advice and this book, in no way overrides any medical advice or medical learning you have been told or have learned.

MY STORY

I recall that when I was planning on bringing a child into this world, I wondered whether my desire to have a baby, was a selfish desire. I was worried about the events taking place all over the world at the time. It seemed that there were so many negative things happening in the world, and I wanted our society, to be a better place to bring a child into. The world seemed like a scary place and from my perspective, things seemed to have got worse, not better.

I have discovered there is a lot of negativity in the world, but there is also an abundance of people wanting to make the world a better place and it is those people that I believe will change the world around us, once and for all. This book is for you, the person ready and willing to make the changes necessary, to grow and develop personally, so that you can guide the children in your care, to become reflective and conscious of their actions and how their decisions impact their own lives and the world around them.

I want to acknowledge all my teachers and role models, who have helped me to create this vision for a better world and who helped to plant the seeds for the 9-PAC Integrity Approach Model and the idea to write this book, on *How to Raise Kids With Integrity*. I also want to acknowledge the people and projects that have helped me to lay the foundation for this book. Stephen Covey and his *The 7 Habits of Highly Effective People*, and The Virtues Project™, have been two of the foundational building blocks that have helped me to create this 9-PAC Integrity Approach Model. Thank you for being the forerunners who created new ideas, words, beliefs and paradigms, who generated an awakening and mindfulness around how we communicate and which words we use with the children in our lives. Words are powerful and they can empower or devalue people. The ancients knew this and their wisdom is coming back into our awareness, through these above models, that speak to us in our time and help us to create a new societal awareness, about the way we role model to children.

This 9-PAC Integrity Approach Model assists all role models, specifically parents, early childcare educators and teachers to communicate in a nurturing, supportive and effective way with the children that they parent and guide. When role models use the 9-PAC Approach, they help children to become consciously aware adults, who can become the change we want to see in our world and help our society to heal and grow into a peaceful community.

When parents, childcare educators and teachers all speak a common empowering language of love, peace and support to our children, nurture them and celebrate their unique skills and abilities, we help them to thrive in their lives and become role models to the people around them. My hope is that if we all are mindful of the 9-PAC Integrity Approach Model, we can become amazing role models for the children we interact with, and assist them to evolve. We can model to the people around us how to guide and communicate with children in an effective and aware way, because what is said to them as a child becomes their inner script and impacts on their self-confidence, sense of self-worth and provides them with the ability to respond to life's tests and challenges with more clarity and inner strength, which, I believe, will contribute to creating a world of peace, harmony and empowerment for all people and life on this planet. I hope you find the model and wisdom it provides in this book inspiring and helpful.

Our behaviour advances our world either positively or negatively and the choices we make individually contribute to the choices that are made collectively. You decide whether to help create empowered role models, who will impact future generations and our society today. You choose to help empower people to become confident in themselves and who make decisions that create positive results, in our families, communities, society and for the planet.

I hope that their wisdom, along with my new role model method, will allow you to open your mind and heart to an awareness of how vital interacting positively with children and people around you impacts our world, so that everyone can see how to become an empowered role model, and teach our children to become tolerant, mindful and accepting adults who treat each other in peaceful and loving ways, thereby forming the utopian society that we all will be proud to live in.

INTRODUCTION

Numerous quotes, scattered throughout the book, along with Stephen Covey's, 'Begin with the End in Mind' habit, which is the second habit from his book, *The 7 Habits of Highly Effective People*, played on my mind over the years, while attending numerous self-development courses. I remember someone asking, "Why didn't we learn this stuff in school?" The 'stuff' they were talking about, is life skills: Planning, Doing, Awareness and Mindfulness.

There are many considerations that we give thought to, when planting a seed or raising an animal. We often seek out advice from those who have gone before us, who had success in the area in which we wish to learn more about. However, in our current society, sometimes there is very little thought given to raising children. Preparation, awareness, compassion and kindness, are the key to raising all living things, whether they be plants, animals or children. This book takes into consideration all the things that are helpful to consider when raising children: positive language, mindfulness, celebrating others differences and reflective decision making. When we role model these traits to our children, they learn to become morally responsible adults, who respect themselves and other people.

CHILDREN
Children learn from watching & role modeling others. Role Models help to create their inner script.

COMMUNITY
We can create supportive, respectful and compassionate communities for our children.

CHARACTER
Children are born with unique skills, traits and talents.

CONSCIOUSNESS
Being reflective of thoughts, actions and beliefs, helps to create mindful children.

How To Raise Children With Integrity

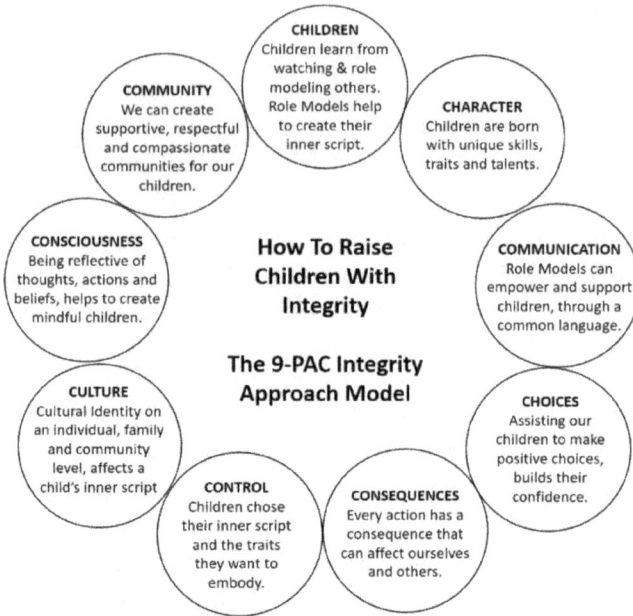

The 9-PAC Integrity Approach Model

COMMUNICATION
Role Models can empower and support children, through a common language.

CULTURE
Cultural Identity on an individual, family and community level, affects a child's inner script

CONTROL
Children chose their inner script and the traits they want to embody.

CONSEQUENCES
Every action has a consequence that can affect ourselves and others.

CHOICES
Assisting our children to make positive choices, builds their confidence.

The 9-PAC Integrity Approach Model:

The 9 Components

Individual (Micro levels)

- Children
- Character
- Communication

Family & Community Level (Sociology levels)

- Choices
- Consequences
- Control

Society and Culture (Macro levels)

- Culture
- Consciousness
- Community

The 9-C groups that I created help parents, childcare educators and teachers learn to raise children with integrity, by learning about and changing the way they interact with children. We start at the individual child level and look at what makes up a child's character traits on a physical, mental, emotional and spiritual level. We dive deep into understanding their how character and personality traits are created, how and why a child's inner script is formed and how role models can make special efforts to notice and celebrate children's unique skills and talents. We focus strongly on Virtues and how they form our inner script and how they can help us to evolve at every 9-C level. The Integrity Approach model then guides us through what type of communication style works best for children and helps to foster confidence, tolerance and compassion in their lives.

In the second tier of the 9-Cs, role models learn how to guide children to make reflective, information-based decisions that take into account the consequences that come with those choices. We discuss how choices not only affect the child, but the people around them and their family units, communities and society. We then look at how consequences can help children learn to have integrity in their daily lives, how control can stifle children, but how too little control or reflections of consequences, can lead to children to become entitled and authoritarian.

In the final tier of the Macro level of the 9-Cs, the book leads us to look at how cultural identity is formed and how it affects a child's inner script, their character, communication style and consciousness. We will explore how role models and children can awaken and become aware of their thoughts, beliefs and actions. We then discuss how it takes a community to raise a child, and how to create a supportive and empowering community, in which children see role models who act and communicate in consistent ways, in all areas of their lives.

I believe that this will help role models to guide children to become the very best versions of themselves in each moment, be able to interact with others to find win–win solutions to our society's problems, becoming leaders and policy makers who use compassion and reflection to make decisions for our society, that take everyone into account and help propel our society into the peaceful place, in which our current and future generations thrive.

Human beings are the most powerful and damaging, tools on this planet. We have the ability to think, speak, create and do, like no other living things on Earth. When we live life as empowered individuals, who authentically embody our unique gifts and talents and who also respect and honour others differences, we contribute to making the world a better place. When we begin to live lives that satisfy our souls and makes us feel complete as individuals, we enhance our communities and our societies and inspire others to adopt our behaviours, which creates a more positive global consciousness.

Yet are we doing this? Can you imagine everyone living life to their fullest potential, or even to the majority of their fullest potential? What could you personally have achieved if you had had the support and guidance of an empowered mentor or role model in your life? What could you have achieved if all your parents, caregivers and educators, had all constantly modelled empowered character traits and spoken a language of support, confidence and compassion to you? How could you have made a difference if you had been taught to use your positive character traits, embody your unique gifts and learned how to change your negative character traits into positive influences?

My intention for this book, is to demonstrate how, when people understand the 9-PAC Integrity Approach, it can help all parents, childcare educators and teachers globally to raise and guide children in a way that brings out the best character traits, not only in them, but also in ourselves. The 9-Cs teach us how to nurture self-confidence, create mindfulness and restore self-awareness in each person and especially with the children we help to guide.

I believe the 9-PAC Integrity Approach can create a world where mindfulness, awareness, compassion, tolerance and encouragement for individuality, innovation and wise choices, and become the norm so everyone functions and acts for the betterment of all living things and for the planet. This I propose, will result in an evolved utopian society, in which we are all proud to live in. Which respects and enhances the quality of life for every living being or organism on the planet.

Children, Character, Communication

We assist our children build their character
through how we communicate with them.

CHAPTER 1

Children

Definition

- a young person

- a son or daughter

- an adult who acts like a child: a childlike or childish person

"If we are to teach real
peace in this world,
and if we are to carry on
a real war against war,
we have to
begin with the children."

Mahatma Gandhi

Little Things

Little drops of water,
Little grains of sand,
Make the mighty ocean
And the pleasant land.

So, the little moments,
Humble though they be,
Make the mighty ages
Of Eternity.

So the little errors
Lead the soul away
From the paths of virtue
Far in sin to stray.

Little deeds of kindness,
Little words of love,
Help to make earth happy
Like the Heaven above.

Julia Abigail Fletcher Carney

Have you ever noticed how a young child's eyes sparkle and shine so brightly? It is said that the eyes are the mirror of the soul and our children are the gifts we give to the world. When we can look at a child and see the wonder in them, the joy and the excitement, we can see their pure potential shining through. They speak truth so easily and are able to see through the deception and our self-limiting beliefs, much more quickly than we can. When we can look at what children can offer us and what they reflect back to us about our own behaviour, we can truly see the gifts that they are, and the gifts they will be, to our future society.

There are many reasons why a person would want to become a parent and why a person would want to become a teacher or childcare educator. In this chapter, we will discuss why people make the choices they do and the importance of role modelling in the life of a child.

Children are not just their physical attributes, they have spiritual, emotional and intellectual aspects as well. When we judge a child based only on their physical characteristics we miss seeing their potential, their talents, their strengths and their ability to grow into amazing individuals who can make positive change in the world.

When we can suspend our judgement, we can create a society of individuals with well-rounded personalities, who embody compassion, kindness and tolerance in their thinking, behaviours and actions. Children see people for who they are and what gifts they can bring to this world. When role models embody this way of thinking, they become people of service to their children, their communities and to their planet.

Children need our guidance to develop these qualities in their own lives. In this chapter, we will discuss how parents, teachers and caregivers can use the 9-PAC (Personal Awareness Components) Integrity Approach Model to become open-minded and compassionate role models for all children.

Enlightened Role Models

When I planned to have a family, I worried about bringing a child into the world and I considered what would happen if my partner or myself were not able to take care of the child. Did I trust either one of us to provide and nurture the child properly? My hope for a brighter future, a kinder and safer world and my faith in humanity, finally enabled me to make the decision to have a child.

Some of us know from very early on that we want to have children, either biological or through adoption. Some people end up parents through an accidental event and some people do not have children of their own, but mentor and nurture the children around them. There are teachers and childcare educators who go into their profession, because they love learning and want to pass this joy onto children. Others may have struggled in school and fell between the cracks, and want to help children who have difficulties learning, to avoid the pain they suffered. Some teachers want to guide and help shape our future citizens and generations.

What some parents and teachers fail to realise is the profound impact having or guiding children has on future generations and the state of our world. Most of us do not consider how having a child, becoming a teacher or being a mentor, will assist in the evolution of humanity or the destruction of our planet. *Children impact our future!* They impact politics, policies and how society functions and makes decisions. They affect how we look after the planet, each other and all the life on it. How an individual role model's personality, character traits, communication styles and actions (your inner script), ultimately impacts how children think and behave (their inner script).

What example are you providing? Are you behaving in a way that you can be proud of? How do you think you will be remembered, from a child's point of view? What character qualities do they see in you? Are you modelling positive traits and behaviours that help others and our society? Are you proud of who you are and your impact on the children around you?

Having children and working with children is the biggest responsibility you are likely to undertake in your life. Whatever behaviours a person models to the next generation is how they will think, how they will act and what they will believe. Are you modelling behaviours that will create the world we all wish to live in? Are you communicating with love, kindness, compassion and using empowering words? Are you helping to create children who lift up society and evolve our systems and institutions? Are you showing children how to care for our planet and life on it? Are you acting as a real mentor?

The 9-PAC Integrity Approach Model believes a real mentor is someone who genuinely wants to see children and others grow and develop into the best possible versions of themselves. They are people who want to help and support others' talents and gifts, so that they can live with purpose and inspire others to also. Being a role model is about appreciating the differences each person has, seeing their innate talents and bringing the best of these gifts to the surface, so that the child you are guiding, can be of service to the world. When you not only celebrate a child's strength of character, but also gently point out ways that they can improve or change their less than ideal character traits, into loving and supportive ones, you can help them to authentically shine.

Being a mentor requires an individual to model diplomacy and 'win–win' decision making strategies. It entails acting with compassion, tolerance and promoting equity in all situations and environments, so that everyone has equal opportunities to succeed and thrive. It is about modelling integrity, honour and the ability to think objectively and 'outside the box'. Being a mentor requires an individual to see obstacles as learning lessons, admit their mistakes and use them as teaching tools. A role model is someone who loves and honours themselves, so they can be of the highest service to the people around them.

It is amazing how fast children learn and adapt their inner script, when they see an adult modelling characteristics that feel good. When they respect a role model, their behaviour and character traits, can change very quickly. What will the world look like in 10, 20, 30 or even 50 years' time? The ironic thing is that rather than worry about what the external world is going to look like, you have the means to create the future you would like to see, by creating a positive inner script within yourself and the children you guide. When you help children to understand how their thoughts affect their actions, and how those actions influence others around them, you help children see how a positive outlook and communication style can help create a safer, more peaceful society. The power is truly within each of us to create positive change through role modelling!

It is my hope that all parents, childcare educators and teachers, can learn to integrate these role model behaviours into their inner script and have positive and compassionate interactions with children and others around them. When people consciously use the 9-PAC Integrity Approach Model, to become the very best role model they can be each day, they create a ripple effect on the people and children around them, who then begin to model these traits and communication styles, to other children and individuals they interact with, which leads to a rapid, positive change in our society.

Physical, Mental, Emotional and Spiritual Elements

Babies and children bring such an immeasurable sense of joy and happiness into our lives. When they are born, they come in to this world as unique individuals. Each has their own distinctive qualities and develops their own skills and talents as they grow. To use an analogy: We are all plants, but we are different types of plants; just as we are all human, one species, but there are many different races and nationalities.

It is easy to see the physical differences in various plant species, just as it is easy to see the physical differences between human beings.

However, children are more than just their physical characteristics, they are a combination of physical, emotional, mental and spiritual characteristics and traits.

The physical aspect of a child is the easiest to notice. When babies are born, we are happy if they are healthy, however, we cannot see with our eyes if everything is functioning normally inside our baby. We may assume that if a child looks fine on the outside, then all is well on the inside. But there is so much more inside each and every one of us, than the physical aspects that we can see on the outside.

People are like icebergs; there is so much beneath the surface that is not obvious. Until you look into the depths of a person's character and inner script and explore their non-physical traits, your assumptions about a person, are often not the whole truth. People can have skills that are non-physical in nature, such as being a fantastic problem solver or having abundant levels of patience. By only focusing on a child's physical attributes, we do not see the emotional, mental and spiritual traits that make up a person's true character. We miss seeing their talents, their gifts and also their inner weaknesses. As role models, we need to cultivate an open-minded and open-hearted approach to 'seeing' the children in our lives for who they are; not only on a physical level, but also on a mental, emotional and spiritual level too.

Many of us know, that we are capable of learning many things and have many thoughts go through our heads on a constant basis, but are those thoughts and beliefs given to us by our parents and caregivers or are they innate beliefs and traits that we are born with? Are we being persuaded to take on someone else's beliefs and thoughts, because we hear something being said regularly? Should we instead understand that the belief is only our parents or caregivers' perspectives and investigate it for ourselves, to make up our own mind, if it suits us and our values?

Can children understand which thoughts are their own and which are their caregiver's thoughts? Can they differentiate between an innate belief that they were born with and a belief they adopted because of hearing it consistently spoken to them? Children between the ages of 0–8 years of age are like sponges. It has been proven that children aged 0–5 absorb information at an amazing rate and their brain function at a genius level during these years. By age five, the brain's level of functioning drops to what we could consider a high level of IQ. By age eight it functions at a normal IQ level.

Very young children must function at this advanced brain level because they have to learn how to function in our world, in order to get their basic needs met. They have to learn how to function in a family environment – to learn to eat, walk, talk, receive love, learn right from wrong and so many other things. Children's inner scripts or set of beliefs, thoughts, perceptions and actions are formed from their parents, caregivers or role models. What they see, they internalise and what they embody into their inner script, they understand to be the correct way to function mentally and emotionally.

This is why it is so important for role models to adopt the 9-PAC Integrity Approach role model system, to guide children. Everything we say and do and the way we behave are recorded into children's minds like a computer system, filed away for later use and pulled out when they need to react to a certain person or situation. For example, if a child sees a parent being compassionate to others around them, irrespective of race or stature, then the child will adopt the same mindset and behaviours. If a child sees a parent or guardian being intolerant of people who are different to them, they will adopt this attitude of intolerance towards anyone who is different than them. If we model empowering behaviours, thoughts and language to the children around us, they will form positive and self-confident inner scripts, which they will use throughout their lives. This script, will be used in their decision-making processes, how they process new information, how they interact with others in groups and how they value our society.

Your mindset is of the utmost importance in becoming a positive role model, as it impacts every part of your life and how you model behaviours and language to children. If your language is negative, this affects your physical, mental, emotional and spiritual mindset and qualities. If your thoughts are negative, this affects how you think and feel about yourself. Most of us have learned to have a negative mindset (inner script) from our parents and caregivers, but also from the people in our community and from society's expectations. If your role model's inner scripts were negative, then that is the inner script you will have learned as a child and are running today, in your mind.

The amazing thing about becoming a 9-PAC role model, is that you can change your mindset with practice, positive thinking and reflection. By continually working to improve your mental, emotional and spiritual qualities, you will help yourself to become emotionally stronger, which will help you in your interactions with others and when life presents you with a lesson to learn. It is entirely possible to change your inner script, no matter what you learned as a child and become the role model you want to be, so that the children around you are able to internalise your positive qualities and understand how to speak to others and interact with them in a positive manner.

People don't become a 9-PAC Integrity Approach role model just to help children, they become this type of positive role model to help everyone around them and to help change our society for the better. This will create a community of people who positively role model thoughts, beliefs and actions for children in their community. These positive scripts will allow these children to achieve amazing things in this world and help to change society as we know it, into a more cohesive and tolerant place to live. The 9-PAC Integrity Approach Model's goal, is to be of service to our children, to society and to humanity, so that we can create a new society, based on positive character traits and beliefs.

We have looked at physical and mental qualities, but what about emotional qualities? They are also learned, as children watch their role models interact with other people. Humans are emotional beings and we all feel joy, love, boredom, sadness and anger. Children watch their role models display emotions and then react in emotional ways. Children go on to treat others in the same way, that they have seen modelled. Monkey see, Monkey do. This can lead a child to understand how to be accepting, loving, encouraging and supportive of other people around them, or it can lead a child to act out in frustration, anger, power plays, violence and other negative behaviours. What you role model, creates either a positive or negative inner script in children. It is important to remember, that you are choosing your child's future by helping a child write his or her inner script and with each emotional decision, action and outburst that you display. Everything we role model creates a ripple effect. You may not think how you behave at home, in school or out in public impacts your child or a child you interact with, but children everywhere are constantly watching us and learning their inner scripts from us.

What can we do to help children change a negative behaviour they learned from us? We can admit to our children that we behaved in an unacceptable way and have discussions with them about how we could have acted in a more appropriate manner. We can ask the child how they would have responded in a similar situation and listen to their response. We might even learn something, from their perspective, if we are open-minded. Each negative emotional outburst we have can be transformed into a learning experience, not only for ourselves, but for our children. The 9-PAC Integrity Approach Model, invites us to be reflective about our own inner script and the behaviours that come from it, so that we can be aware of what we do and why. When we role model that we can change our inner script, we show children that is it okay to change their inner scripts as well and it empowers everyone to grow and evolve.

By choosing to act from the 9-PAC Integrity Approach Model principles, you will be able to role model in a way that helps children to enhance their emotional qualities and helps them grow into emotionally stable and balanced future citizens. The model can be used to help you to support children to find their own way in the world, by helping them to embody love, optimism and joy, so they can feel free to truly be themselves and encourage others to do the same.

Freedom can allow a person to act from their authentic self, meaning the innate qualities they were born with. We are all born with inherent spiritual qualities, some are obvious, while others are not so obvious. Spiritual qualities are the characteristics that we all have within us, that make us feel good about ourselves. The spiritual qualities that the 9-PAC Integrity Approach Model focuses on are: kindness, respect, thoughtfulness, consideration, compassion, generosity, helpfulness, gentleness, gratitude, understanding, friendliness and courtesy. By becoming a 9-PAC role model, you work to embody these spiritual qualities in your daily life, so that you can nurture yourself and the children around you.

These spiritual qualities help us grow into the person that we want to become. They make our soul sing when we think, act, and behave from these characteristics. Being mindful of your spiritual qualities, helps you to decide what actions to take, in both good and challenging times. You always have a choice on how to react and therefore how to behave. Being mindful of your spiritual qualities and choosing a path that includes these qualities, is what the 9-PAC Integrity Approach Model considers to be the road to happiness. I believe that everyone wants to experience peace and joy in their lifetime, not just fleetingly, but to continuously feel these things in their life. This requires us all to work consistently to fully embody these spiritual qualities, through self-awareness and self-development. Many of us are aware of these spiritual qualities, but may not have grown up having them modelled to us, so they may be missing from our inner script. We may long to embody them in our lives, but we find that negativity and deep wounds, have prevented us from living these spiritual qualities, to their fullest potential. The most wonderful thing about the 9-PAC Integrity Approach Model, is you can ALWAYS change your inner script, by working through your blocks and choosing to mindfully practice these spiritual qualities, each and every day.

Children in your care may have been wounded by you, by a parent or by the caregivers in their lives, but they can also change their inner scripts and learn to embody positive spiritual traits by watching you role model them. No one is *ever* stuck in a concrete inner script. They always have the choice to change their script, but often don't know how to do that, or are in an environment where they are not able to see anyone model these positive qualities. That is why I am wrote this book. It is my dearest hope that parents, teachers and caregivers use the 9-PAC Integrity Approach Model, not only to change their inner script, but to help children change their inner scripts, by embodying the positive qualities we model to them.

Regardless of how obvious these qualities are in each child or person you encounter, you are now aware of how your role modelling can affect and empower others. I believe the most important spiritual qualities are gratitude, having an open mind and an open heart. Practicing gratitude contributes to a positive open mindset and having an open mind reinforces the trait of being accepting of others. As we realise that other people have different frames of reference than we do, we understand that we can all learn from each other, no matter what our differences are. Having an open heart reminds us that we are all connected as human beings and that whatever we say to someone affects their beliefs, emotions, and mindset.

For example, if a teacher were to encourage a spiritual quality each week, the class could discuss how that quality could be displayed in their actions, thoughts and behaviours throughout the week. If 'respect' was the theme of the week and children were given five minutes each morning to suggest ways that respect could be practiced, it would make them consciously aware of when respect was being displayed around them. Children could model respect, by listening to each other without interrupting and by treating others with courtesy. They would be able to consciously acknowledge these behaviours as respectful, through their daily five-minute reflection. At the end of the week, the teacher could ask students to share their experiences, of how they practiced respect throughout the week to others, how it felt to be respected or not be respected, and how they could show more respect in their families, communities and society. Students could then share ideas that they gained from their reflection time, with the rest of the class, which would help inspire other children. Parents can also practice this example at home, during dinner time, after school or after a play date.

We as role models need to be aware that not all children have a home life that is ideal, so it is essential that their other key role models outside of the home contribute to the child's spiritual growth. There are three main crucial areas where children need role models in their life when they are young: parents, childcare educators, and their primary school teachers. If a child is raised with praise and empowered in all three areas, they will grow to have an empowered and positive inner script and become the type of citizen that we wish to have in our communities and have running our countries. These children would embody all of the 9-PAC Integrity Approach Model qualities and consistently use them in all of their interactions with people around them. When future generations of adults choose to role model having a loving and open heart, I believe it will make a positive difference and make the world a better place for us all to live in.

Being of Service to Our Children

The first question to ask one's self as a parent is, "What is my intention in raising my child? What do I want my family to look like in 20 years' time? Who do I want my child to grow up to be?" When I pose these questions to you, are you thinking about your child's career? Do you want them to become a doctor, a nurse, an engineer? Or are you thinking about which character qualities you would like them to develop, such as becoming a morally and socially responsible adult? Do you want to raise a child who is kind, caring and respectful of others and their opinions, even if they differ from their own and who acts in a way that contributes to making the world a better place?

As a parent, childcare educator or teacher, you are the role model of what a grown up looks like, how they behave and how they think. There is a small percentage of children who have a massive impact on the world right now, but in the future, when our children have grown into adults, every single child will have greater influence due to having voting rights, being in the workforce and contributing to society by raising future generations. You, as their mentor, have significant influence in what the future looks like, for our children and our future society. Your position in a child's life is so much more important than you may realise.

"Children are our most precious commodity, as they are our future."

Babies become toddlers, toddlers become primary and middle school children, who then become high school students and grow into young adults. They go on to become employees, business owners, teachers, parents, leaders and possibly politicians, who direct our society and create the systems it functions within. They are the ones who will determine what our approaching years will look like and what behaviour is and isn't acceptable in our future society. They will determine the rules of society, our economy, the problems we have in our communities and how we deal with problems. They will conclude how our justice system operates, whether or not it is equitable, and to what degree corruption is condoned.

Having children and teaching children is a massive responsibility that becomes a life path of serving others. Our role modelling will create a future generation who learn to role model the positive traits we taught them to their children. You can change how you parent, teach and role model, by the aware and heart-centred 9-PAC Integrity Approach Model, that encourages children's gifts and talents while empowering the child with knowledge about how to respond to people around them in positive ways. You have an opportunity to enhance a child's emotional stability and their sense of self-worth.

During childhood years, it is vital that we assist children to develop and access their higher-self wisdom, their compassion and their ability to work openly and positively with other people. By helping them discover their authentic self in early childhood and by teaching them how to compassionately and effectively cope with various situations in life, you can help them learn how to overcome difficulties and develop the skills they will need, to negotiate the trials and obstacles they will face in life. Although the issues that they face as a child may seem minor to us, such as fighting over a toy, their situation is very real to them and by having effective and compassionate coping skills, a happy resolution for all parties involved is achieved, and a lifelong skill in dealing with conflict is discovered and established.

For example, if a role model sees two children arguing over a toy, the role model could speak to the children about what characteristics they are displaying, whether they are positive or negative and how they think their behaviour is affecting the other child. The person could ask the children how they want the other child to behave, so that it would make them feel good as well as making the other child feel good. The child might say something such as, "It's not fair that they took my toy and it made me feel sad." The person could explore this with the child who took the toy and speak about sharing and how sharing makes everyone feel valued. They could ask the child if they can come up with a solution to the problem that would be fair to everyone involved. The role model, could ask the child who had their toy taken, if they could have done anything to prevent the argument from happening? How they could find ways to share more effectively and make the other child feel included? If we take the time to listen to children and their opinions of the event and how they viewed the event, rather than telling them what to do, how to behave or just getting angry with them, we help them find their own answers and create positive solutions and develop problem solving skills.

People and children want to tell their experiences, from their perspective, as it is the perspective that is most important to them. Once they feel heard and acknowledged, most individuals will be open to hearing others' perspectives, as long as there is a role model moderating the discussion who can help all parties involved, to view the situation from a shared perspective. A role model in this situation, will create a compassionate and supportive space, in which to have this discussion and once everyone has been heard, it is much easier for all of the people involved to reflect on how they could do things in a more positive way. This is because they allowed themselves to see something from someone else's perspective, they can feel compassion for the other person. Once compassion is created, reflection is possible. It is then a good time to thank the children for their ability to be open-minded and for the thoughtfulness and compassion that they showed each other and for taking the time to come up with a solution, that both parties can be happy with.

Parents and educators can help a child to learn these positive traits by first educating themselves on how to be good role models, who are of service to children.

Some skills 9-PAC Integrity Approach role models can seek to embody are:

- Keeping an open mind
- Engage in a willingness to constantly keep learning
- Having the flexibility to make the changes you deem necessary in your life
- Cultivating the self-discipline, in order to create healthy habits
- Having confidence in yourself, to take the next courageous step, that life wants you to take, in order to become the person, you were meant to be

You are in the driver's seat. You are in control of your destination and the remodelling of your inner script. The 9-PAC Integrity Approach Model believes that it is vital that you role model the behaviour and language to children that you want to see them use in our world.

When you, as an individual consciously choose to be a role model and you are aware of your behaviour, your words and the impact they have on others, you are more likely to help children around you create compassionate and respectful inner scripts. When you role model these behaviours to children, they have better interactions and form stronger relationships, with their family members and people in their communities. When individuals use positive scripts to interact with each other, it reduces confrontations and instead allows people to listen to each other's ideas and create innovative solutions in a peaceful and compassionate environment. When people use positive scripts not only in their homes but in schools, communities, businesses and in society, this will positively impact our world in numerous ways. When society models these positive scripts, our communities, consciousness and culture, will all change to become the peaceful, innovative and mindful place we desire them to be.

The 9-PAC Integrity Approach Model helps us to understand how a person's character is created and looks at how character traits impact a person's personality, strengths and weaknesses. In the next chapter, we will discuss how to identify positive characteristics in children, how to help them evolve their positive traits and how to help them shift their negative traits, so they can evolve into more well-rounded individuals.

CHAPTER 1 – SUMMARY

- The goal is to become an enlightened role model

- We help to create future leaders, through parenting, caring for and teaching children

- Role models must look beyond a child's physical attributes to 'see' their emotional, spiritual and mental abilities as well

- Role models live 'in service' to our children

- 9-PAC Integrity Approach Model empowers our children to change their inner script through watching role models, change their own inner scripts

- Being a role model requires us to continually learn and improve our own scripts and qualities

CHAPTER 2

Character

Definition

- The way someone thinks, feels, and behaves: someone's personality

- A set of qualities that are shared by many people in a group, country, etc.

- A set of qualities that make a place or thing different from other places or things

"You must be the change
that you want to see in
this world."

Mahatma Gandhi

**A list of characteristics from The Virtues Project™
Reflections Cards:**

Acceptance	Faithfulness	Orderliness
Accountability	Fidelity	Patience
Appreciation	Flexibility	Peacefulness
Assertiveness	Forbearance	Perceptiveness
Awe	Forgiveness	Perseverance
Beauty	Fortitude	Purity
Caring	Friendliness	Purposefulness
Certitude	Generosity	Reliability
Charity	Gentleness	Resilience
Cheerfulness	Grace	Respect
Cleanliness	Gratitude	Responsibility
Commitment	Helpfulness	Reverence
Compassion	Honesty	Righteousness
Confidence	Honour	Sacrifice
Consideration	Hope	Self-Discipline
Contentment	Humanity	Serenity
Cooperation	Humility	Service
Courage	Idealism	Simplicity
Courtesy	Independence	Sincerity
Creativity	Initiative	Steadfastness
Decisiveness	Integrity	Strength
Detachment	Joyfulness	Tact
Determination	Justice	Thankfulness
Devotion	Kindness	Thoughtfulness
Dignity	Love	Tolerance
Diligence	Loyalty	Trust
Discernment	Mercy	Trustworthiness
Empathy	Mindfulness	Truthfulness
Endurance	Moderation	Understanding
Enthusiasm	Modesty	Unity
Excellence	Nobility	Wisdom
Fairness	Openness	Wonder
Faith	Optimism	Zeal

Character traits make up our personality and are created by what a person thinks, believes and feels. They are a person's actions, perceptions, opinions, patterns and are all influenced by a person's inner script. Character traits influence how an individual communicates, the tone they use, their body language and their level of confidence, that they portray. An individual's character is also made up of their physical, mental, emotional and spiritual qualities. Our personalities are a mix of many character traits, both inherent to us from when we were born and learned characteristics, from watching our caregivers, parents, teachers and friends, role model their character traits to us.

In this chapter, we will discuss how character is formed and that our character is a choice, both in how we choose our character and our attitude. We will introduce The Virtues Project™, and look at how our character impacts others and the children around us. I will show how we can choose to embody more spiritual characteristics, in order to help us become better role models. We will take a look at how virtues affect our character and our ability to effectively role model. When we have a strong sense of our own character, we can become confident and compassionate leaders, that become empowered role models for our children.

The Virtues Project™

The Virtues Project™ is one of the best programs I have come across. It teaches what I consider to be the most effective way of communicating with others, via strategies which help individuals build their self-esteem and raise their awareness. It also helps individuals to understand how their behaviour impacts their life and the lives of those around them. The Virtues Project™ helps to contribute to an individual's understanding of their moral compass and how challenges in their lives have assisted them in growing spiritually stronger and more emotionally stable. The Virtues Project™ is a program that speaks the language, that we so desperately need in our society: A language of caring, compassion, empathy, discernment, faith, hope, responsibility, reliability, commitment, helpfulness, love, unity and so much more. I believe that if virtues are generally missing from our society because they are missing from our language.

The Virtues Project™ was created by a psychotherapist, a child psychologist and Disney imagineer, who together came up with five strategies for communicating, using virtues. One of the founders had an interest in religion and discovered that every religion had a common thread of virtues: kindness, compassion, acceptance, tolerance, love and respect. Whether the people who are reading this book are religious or not, we all have these spiritual qualities inherent within us and most people value these qualities in others. As in everything in life, it is best to keep an open mind and take what you can from other people's discoveries; that is wisdom in practice. As you explore the strategies of The Virtues Project™, take from it the parts that resonate with you, and leave the rest. The Virtues Project™ purpose was to help reduce violence, racism and other negative behaviours in the world and the more people that contribute to that goal, the faster we will achieve it.

Learning to understanding the reasons people do the things they do is fascinating to me. One of the first personal development courses I attended, was focused on The Virtues Project™. I became a Master Facilitator, as the language that they used spoke to me very deeply. I am very passionate about the language we use, as it shapes our character and ultimately shapes our society and the world around us. The Virtue Project list of virtues at the beginning of this chapter, helped me to begin to form a set of foundation words, for my 9-PAC Integrity Approach Model.

In the Virtues Project™ every virtue relates to another virtue. It is said you can't practice one virtue without another and when you think about it, it is difficult to isolate virtues on their own, without first seeing how other virtues are practiced. The more an individual opens their mind, the more they learn to see themselves and others around them as holistic beings, not just people with compartmentalised emotions and behaviours that get displayed, depending on the environment they are in. A person who has a strong character, may be loud, gregarious, fair, smart, objective, passionate, driven, forceful and even egotistical. These character traits are not isolated things on their own, they all tie into one another; to make up the person's personality, beliefs, thoughts and perceptions of the world. The person with the strong character and the person who is the worrier, will have totally different personalities, beliefs, thoughts and perceptions, even though they may share some similar character traits.

To be a positive role model, we all need to consistently reflect on our own thoughts, actions and behaviours and the children that we guide, and begin to understand each virtue and how we perceive it, what it means to us and how it fits into the whole, in order to understand how virtues make up a complete personality.

When you look at the virtues list think about what your strength virtues are and which ones you would like to embody more, and which ones your friends, family and children around you have. Look at each virtue and see how it makes you feel, what your perceptions, beliefs and thoughts are when you read them. Do you immediately think of someone when you read a certain virtue? What do you think about them? Does someone else you know have the same virtue, but you see them in a totally different way? There are no right or wrong answers to this exercise. It is simply a reflective exercise to become aware of your perceptions, thoughts and beliefs around the virtues list. Each person reading this book will see the list differently and have different emotional responses to each of the virtues. The point of the exercise is for you to become aware of what you think these words mean to you, and begin to understand how they can form a holistic personality.

We all have character traits or virtues that as we look at the list, we can pick them out and say, "Yes, I have those traits or I embody and act out those traits." These traits shape our personality, how we interact with people, respond to them and how we behave during events in our life. If we go deeper into the virtues, we can notice that **we do possess all of these virtues**! Yes, each of us possesses each of these virtues, but we may only practice them in certain situations or maybe only later in life, when we have become more mindful and self-reflective. Some virtues are harder to practice than others. We may not even be aware we have all these virtues in our personalities, but others see them in us. For example, a child may not see that they have the virtue of mindfulness, but their teacher sees it in their actions regarding their schoolwork or behaviour. Some virtues are very obvious in certain personalities, but harder to see clearly in others. We may only consciously embody 20% or 50% of the virtues on the page. We might be able to say we embody more of them, but do not do showcase them all on a consistent basis. Maybe we look at the list at the beginning of this chapter and wish we did embody some of these traits daily and wish that we could use them to improve our character and our lives.

When we look at the virtues list, we may also see that our spouse, co-worker, friend or parent, embodies some of the traits that we think we don't have. We acknowledge that we appreciate them for having these character traits or maybe we even resent them for having the traits that we wish we had.

The virtues listed, shows us that mindfully focussing on small actions or traits can have massive impacts. Looking at these virtues, reflecting on them and 'feeling' into the beliefs and ideas you have about them, has a more positive impact than you realise.

When you can look at a virtue and see how you use it or don't use it in your life, how you feel about it, who you know who has that trait and how you think and feel about them, you begin to understand the framework of your own personality, perceptions, beliefs, language and inner script that you are taking on board in your life.

Through the virtues list, it is reasoned that everyone is unique, that everyone is special and that many of the virtues that I myself did not pick, I acknowledge to be someone else's virtues. I learned to understand through The Virtues Project™, that I could become more compassionate and tolerant of other people's virtues and see them as strengths of character, instead of difference that I might not understand or care for. I realised that everyone is on a spiritual journey and that we are all at different stages of development and we are all role models for each other. For example, I may not like the sacrifice virtue that I see in a co-worker. I may see it as a detrimental personality trait, but if I look deeper and see that this is only my perception of the word and that it comes from my own experiences and belief systems, I can begin to see how it might be a strength of character for that other person.

All virtues can be seen in a positive and also negative light, but if we learn to be open minded to each virtue and begin to see them as a potential positive strength of character in people's personalities, we can help guide people, especially the children in our care, on how to enhance these virtues into strengths of character in their personalities. If the virtue they have in their inner script is not a strength of character, we can help the child to become aware of the detrimental effects of the virtue in their life, and help them shift this virtue into a more positive aspect. For example when attending my first virtue's workshop, I was staying with an aunt of mine who was reminiscing about when I was younger and proceeded to tell me about a particular memory and then stated that I was a very stubborn child. I instantly recognised that as a child I was determined rather than stubborn and saw the positive perspective.

Building character is something that happens all the time, whether we recognise it or not. It is built through watching our caregivers, parents, teachers, childcare educators, family, friends, people in our community and in our society, act and behave. It is built through challenging situations that we face. They shape our thoughts, ideas, beliefs and our inner and outer dialogue and actions.

Each person builds their character by choosing what they believe in, which results in how they behave.

You may look at this above sentence and may not agree with it, but have you ever seen an adult model a behaviour that you did not agree with, and you decided you did not want to be like them? This is you consciously choosing not to embody the character trait that you saw being role modelled. Our internal script was formed when we were children, which in turn helped us to determine our actions. It was formed by watching the role models around us interact with each other and other people in our communities. Many of our own character traits are not inherent to the personality we had, when we were born; they are learned character traits. For example, many people are unconscious of the internal script and the character traits and virtues that they display, until they begin to reflect on their own inner script and character, and see which character traits they have adopted in childhood. A person may not have come into this world with the virtue of intolerance or manipulation, but they have learned that behaviour from their parents or people in their community. However, everyone has the ability to become mindful of their character traits, which ones they want to enhance and which ones they wish to change.

Virtues guide you to live your life to its fullest potential and to become the best person you can be. Virtues feel good, when put into action, virtues can challenge you to become the person you want to be and to be the change you want to see in the world. By attending a Virtues Project™ workshop I learnt one of their strategies is 'The Language of The Virtues' which enables us to embody these traits into identities so that we can also honour, encourage and celebrate the positive virtues that we see in ourselves and others that we admire. We can embody the positive virtues that we see others role modelling, that we want to display in our own personalities. I invite you to personally select a virtue to practice on a daily basis, to increase your ability to express what you want from life and how you expect to be treated – such as kindness, compassion or respect. You can also do this exercise with your children, class or colleagues. Additionally you can participate in the global 'Virtue of the Week' (www.ethicalfoundations.com.au) and contribute to the wider global consciousness. The Virtue of the Week makes us mindful of how we choose to treat people including ourselves. Developing our self-awareness and putting our virtues into action helps us to become comfortable with who we are and supports us through the challenges we have in life. Virtues support us by helping us learn how to respond with integrity to difficult situations and gives us a better understanding of other people's characteristics and personality traits.

By selecting a virtue every day or each week, you become aware of how it affects your relationships, your emotional state, your confidence and how it helps you assist others in developing their confidence and self-worth. As 9-PAC Integrity Approach role models for children, we need to notice the virtues they embody and model the virtues we would like children to learn. For example, if a child displays loyalty, empathy and optimism, we as parents, early childcare educators and teachers would acknowledge these wonderful traits. We would celebrate them and encourage them and we would help the student learn to model these virtues to others around them. If we see that that student would benefit from having the accountability trait, we can speak to them about what this trait means, help them learn how to think it, be mindful of practicing it, help them learn how to speak it and then role model that behaviour for them consistently ourselves.

To help a child understand the accountability virtue, we might talk about how being accountable with their homework is a very important trait to have and how it can help them down the road to succeed in their jobs, on sports teams and in life. We would detail how it can help them in their life now and in the future, by giving them examples. You might say to a Grade 4 student, "Accountability can help you with your homework, by helping you to realise that you are accountable to me, your teacher and your group project classmates, to do your part of the project. If you are not accountable, there will be consequences for these actions and they might include your group receiving a bad mark, your group members being upset with you, and you having to explain to your teacher, why you did not do the work."

You could speak to them about words that describe accountability such as:

- self-discipline – controlling your mind and body

- assertiveness – taking action to get your work done on time

- compassion – caring about the other group members and their desire to do well

- diligence – which is practicing doing 'First Things First' by Stephen Covey, or in the language of the virtues: perseverance, commitment, and steadfastness, so that you don't get distracted and forget to do the assignment.

By explaining the word accountability, you have not only spoken it, you have helped the child to understand the word and to think mindfully about the word. You can now help them use the word and the words that describe it when they write in their notebooks or journal. You can help them speak it to you, when you ask them about how the project is going. You can celebrate and acknowledge when they use the words and display accountability, in regard to their project or at any other moment you recognise it in their behaviour. You can role model accountability in your own behaviour and speak words of accountability when you give their projects back to them or give them a new assignment.

What you are doing is helping them to learn a common language, that will help them to nurture self-confidence and self-awareness within themselves and to learn to embody a new virtue. When they think, speak and act out a new virtue consistently, they cause it to become part of their consciousness. This causes it, over time, to become a subconscious behaviour. A subconscious behaviour is something that a person does not have to think about doing, they just do it because it is part of their personality. This forms part of their personal integrity as they find their inner strength.

When you grow in self-awareness, it builds your confidence and assists humanity to evolve, advance and progress, by creating ethical foundations in and for our children and ourselves, to excel from. We can all obtain a sense of fulfilment and love for our fellowman, by understanding all of the virtues and by using them daily, so that we begin to embody them into our personalities.

It is the goal of the 9-PAC Integrity Approach Model – that virtues be used to guide and be role modelled to others around us. Enabling personality traits and character traits when modelled consistently, creates a ripple effect that begins to make change in our families, communities, cities, countries, societies and out into the world. The more people who observe virtues being displayed, the more people will seek to also display these positive characteristics that they see being modelled and change begins to happen all around us.

Role modelling positive character traits is something that can be done, not only on a parent/child level or teacher/student level, it can be modelled parent/parent, parent/community member, parent/teacher, teacher/parent, student/student, teacher/teacher, administrator/teacher, board/administrator and child/parent and child/teacher. We can learn from the positive virtues that children around us display as well! It can be used for sports teams, after-school organisations, community programs, clubs, businesses, religious organisations, political and city divisions and can be used from a micro to a macro level in all areas of society.

By focussing on a characteristic to further develop or a virtue, it creates the aim to live mindfully by that virtue for the day. Many people react unconsciously to circumstances and situations they find themselves in, rather than being mindfully aware of their conduct. For example if someone was focussing on the virtue of being helpful, on that particular day, they may think, "Today I am going to be as helpful to as many people today as I can." This sets up a positive attitude for the day, regardless of what they face during the course of it. It will also positively impact how they treat others.

Discussing with children the daily virtue they saw being practiced, how they felt about the virtue, and if they noticed that this virtue was missing from their observations or own actions, supports children in learning to be mindful of if they want this virtue to be become part of their life internally and externally. They consciously begin to create the world that they would like to live in, by using their discernment and practicing the virtues that they want to see in the world. Regardless of their age, children can understand emotions and feelings, that are both positive and negative. This can help them to understand what virtues they want to have and which ones they don't want to have, in their inner script and personality.

When we all work to speak the 9-PAC Integrity Approach Model's common language of positive virtues, we learn to support, encourage and celebrate others and their differences. When we help each other consistently practice these traits and to teach each other how to speak and integrate positive characteristics into our internal script, this will help to create a society of people who all strive to become the very best and most compassionate, balanced and tolerant they can be and to help other achieve the same level of success. These are the building blocks for a utopian society.

Personality Tools

Now that we know what virtues are, how do we know which virtues we have in our own personalities? There are many things that contribute to our personality and some people have compartmentalised these into specific, yet generalised, character traits. There are a few personality tests such as the Myers–Briggs Personality Type Indicator (MBTI) where there are 16 MBTI types. You determine your preference for four areas, such as whether you feel you are an extrovert or an introvert, how you believe you interpret information, what you like to consider when making decisions and what degree of structure you like in your life. These four choices will determine which of the 16 MBTI types you are.

What I have learned throughout my life, that even though you may fit into one 'box', at one stage of your life, it can change, as you change. This is the reason they do not encourage businesses to use this for the purpose of selecting employees. I have met people who do not fit the profile their job requires, but because of their personal belief, passion and ability to view matters on a larger scale, they consciously choose to act differently to what their personality preferences are listed as. Beliefs and passion cannot be measured and this is the reason I encourage open hearts and open minds, so that people who are passionate about certain issues and topics in the world will not be overlooked, because they do not meet a personality test, that some organisation wishes to implement.

Discovering that someone in a group is the opposite of you and understanding what gifts they bring and what gifts you bring to a discussion or purpose, encourages cooperation and unity in ensuring that all angles are considered when working together with a common purpose. This is the reason it is important to see the gifts that we all bring to the table, rather than see our differences as something that is looked down upon. If children started to see how each of them is unique and that their differences are a gift to the world, imagine what future businesses and organisations could achieve! Children would also not be as likely to bully others.

Another perspective of personality profiles, is the DISC Profile, which is a system for personality analysis, based on four main areas that determine whether you are more task- or people orientated-person, or whether you have a more active or passive style of behaviour. DISC educates you about your general characteristics, your value to a team, possible weaknesses and your greatest fear. The letters in DISC stand for Dominant/Driver, Influencing/ Inspiring, Compliant/Correct, Stable/Steady.

Gary Chapman shared another perspective with us and has written numerous books about 'The Five Love Languages', which states that there are five main love languages throughout the world and that we all have one or two preferred ways of showing love and feeling loved. The five love languages are:

1. Physical Touch

2. Words of Affirmation

3. Quality Time

4. Gifts

5. Acts of Service

The interesting thing is, that although we may feel that we are showing our partner or children that we love them, we are speaking to them in our love language, not theirs and they are not feeling the love that we are giving; because we are speaking a different language. If we were to listen or observe how they show love to us, we would learn how they want to be loved. A wife's preferred language might be acts of service so she feels loved when her husband works alongside her each evening until everything is done and they can relax together. The husband's preferred language might be words of affirmation so he likes to hear words of support and encouragement. This relationship can have a downside, if the husband tells his wife how wonderful she is, but she is not hearing it, as she is not feeling the love because he is not working alongside her each evening. She starts to criticise him and this causes him to not feel loved. It is the same with children, we need to give them love in the way that they are sharing it, which once you have opened your mind and learned about the five love languages, you will view their actions from a different perspective, then you may have previously. A child who interrupts their parents or teacher to give them a flower or drawing, is showing their love through gifts, while another child is happy to sit quietly on a parent lap, because they feel love through physical touch.

Lominger is another tool based on leadership development and has numerous competencies, which also include virtues such as compassion, creativity, humour, integrity, perseverance and trust. It also includes other areas of competence, such as motivating others, priority setting, problem solving, ethics and values and so much more.

Another perspective is Edward de Bono's, Six Thinking Hats theory, where he promotes looking at issues from six different angles in order to make a decision; so that you can have considered all potential outcomes. The six hats and areas of consideration are:

1. White hat – information known or needed

2. Red hat – feelings, hunches and intuition

3. Black hat – judgement – being the devil's advocate and why something may not work

4. Yellow hat – brightness and optimism

5. Green hat – creativity – the possibilities, alternatives and new ideas

6. Blue hat – to manage the thinking process

Understanding our personality traits can help us to understand that we are all unique. When we learn about our own personality type category, it helps us to discover our strengths and our weaknesses and to understand these traits in a more mindful way. When we can see what personality traits we think and behave from, we are more able to consciously choose to either enhance these traits or evolve them until they are more balanced. We can even choose to embody new traits, that are not inherent to us, but that we might want to embody, after learning more about them. For example, in our own personality test, we may see that we are quiet, serious, dependable, practical, matter-of-fact and responsible. We may however, want to add in the traits of friendly and conscientious, to our personality mix, in order to be a more well-rounded individual. Knowing all the personality types can help us to create our own personality mix, that fits us the best and allows us to become the best version of ourselves that we can be.

If teachers and childcare educators have an awareness of various personality types, they are better able to be more accepting of their students and colleagues and understand how to communicate with each child and work together for the purpose of serving future generations. The teacher or childhood educator would know what each child's potential personality group might be, and could help that child to enhance their positive characteristics and become mindful of the traits they need to strengthen, that are inherent to the child's personality group. They could help them to evolve or change their internal script, and to enhance those traits, to become more balanced. Parents could also learn these personality groups to help them better understand their children and their partner. This would enable them to understand how to communicate on a deeper level with their child and partner, and how to role model in a way, that would be understood by each person. It would allow positive traits, to be more readily adapted into each person's inner scripts. These personality group types, can help us appreciate our children, partners and students, for who they are, and the strengths and skills that they bring into our lives and into the world.

Life would be quite boring if we were all the same and we learn the most, from people who have opposite personality traits to us. This is because it forces us to stretch our minds and our comfort zones and become more tolerant and mindful of other's thoughts, beliefs and actions. It opens our eyes to things we may never have considered before, because we have a tendency to become comfortable and only see the world from our own inner script. Realising that everyone has a different inner script, virtues, personality types, skills and gifts is key to understanding that all these components are essential in this world and that without the gifts and skills of other people, we would be unable to fulfil our own purpose, to the best of our ability. For example, a child who wants to understand what motivates people and is insightful about others, would be wonderful in a group situation. A child who has an original mind and a great drive for implementing their ideas and achieving their goals, would also be a huge asset to the group. Both children together in the same group, would complement each other and allow for a more well-rounded project to be created and also the creation of a better group atmosphere. The goal-oriented child will make sure that ideas get accomplished and the empathic child would make sure that everyone was heard and felt acknowledged.

Character is a Choice

When we neglect to help our children become mindful of their personality traits, we deprive them of the ability to know who they are and which qualities make up their personality. We limit their understanding, of both their strengths and their weaknesses, which causes them to have less respect for their own thoughts, feelings and decisions. This may result in them become a 'follower' of someone who they perceive as having a stronger personality. When we fall short of teaching them to respect their own intuition and to have the courage to walk away or not participate in actions or behaviours that could have a negative effect on their mind or body, we open up the potential that they may follow a path that could be detrimental to their present and future life. When our children are young, they may be encouraged to do things that they are not comfortable with, such as bullying, being encouraged to try a particular substance such as alcohol or drugs or engage in an experience such as stealing or participating in forced sexual activity. By failing to inform and discuss with our children, the potential implications that certain behaviours are likely to have on their life and the people around them, we contribute to the negative issues which are prevalent in our society today.

As 9-PAC Integrity Approach role models, we should empower the children around us, to help them have the best chance for success and to live their life to its fullest potential. A role model is a life coach, in essence. As our children grow and we help them to maintain a positive mindset, their confidence positively affects how they interact with others, which in turn helps this world to become a better place for us all to live in. There are already amazing children who make incredible differences in the world, because of their sense of service to others. 9-PAC Integrity Approach role models look for virtues in everyone, to see what their strengths are, how their inherent personality virtues can be utilised in positive ways and help children to try out new virtues that they might want to include in their inner script.

We have all heard of people who were told by parents or teachers, that they would never amount to anything, yet they grew up to become role models, innovators and entrepreneurs who found their purpose in life and became happy, well-rounded individuals, who contributed to society in important ways. How did they turn out that way, when someone in a role model position told them they were not worthy? They choose to embrace their strengths and weakness and bring out the best of their personality qualities and virtues. This shows that a person's inner script, personality and behaviour is a choice. All it takes for a person to overcome the difficulties around them is to become mindful of what their positive traits and virtues are and work to make them shine.

The goal of 9-PAC Integrity Approach Model is to encourage parents, teachers and childcare educators, to use compassionate and empowering language, employ mindfulness techniques and help children become aware of their virtues and personality traits. The more we understand virtues and personality types on a deep level, the more comfortable we are in seeing these traits in ourselves and in others. We can be mindful of our thoughts, feelings, compassion and tolerance, because we are aware of what types of virtues and personalities there are in the world and how to interact with them. Then we can appreciate other's differences and work with them, as we grow and develop spiritually, emotionally and intellectually.

When we view things from different perspective than our own inner script, we form new understandings of how others view the world. It is said that once you learn something, you can never unlearn it and when we are able to see all virtues as strengths of character, we are better able to role model and empower children. Knowing what your strengths and weaknesses are, actually strengthens you. People often view our physical weakness and assume they are also our mental, emotional and spiritual weakness. However, there are many people who are amazing examples of how this is not always the case. For example, Christopher Reeve, an American actor who played Superman, became a quadriplegic after a horse-riding injury. His paralysis did not stop him from expanding his positive character traits and being of service to the world, as he went onto become an activist for people with spinal cord injuries and for human embryonic stem cell research; founding research centres and charitable foundations.

As we work to bring out the best qualities of our virtues, we discover that what was once a weakness, becomes one of our strengths. Any changes we make continually and intentionally gradually strengthens our weaknesses, whether they be physical, mental, emotional or spiritual. As we build up our virtues and character traits, we feel good about who we are and how we are showing up in the world. When we take the time to discover our own weaknesses and work to improve upon them, we are much better able to help others creatively and compassionately, to work on their weaknesses. The 9-PAC Integrity Approach is not about forcing people into acting in certain ways, it is about helping everyone enhance and learn how to empower themselves through their own gifts, talents and skills, through gentle guidance and individual reflection, as all the answers to our problems are within us.

Attitude

The 9-PAC Integrity Approach Model views attitude as an essential piece to creating a positive character. A person's character will be tested, tried, built, broken, enhanced and tested again. Attitude is a choice, as well as a characteristic. Every chapter within this book is interrelated, just like a person's life. A person's attitude and choices affect so many different aspects of their life and affects the way a person sees their own virtues and personality. A person chooses their own attitude, because nobody else can force a permanent attitude on another person. You get to decide the attitude you choose to embody in this life and therefore, that attitude colours each and every aspect of your life. A person's attitude impacts their family, friends, colleagues, neighbours, clients, patients and their children. Children are particularly susceptible to a role model's attitude, because they are still learning, that they have a choice on what type of attitude they want to cultivate. What type of attitude do you think will help create positive future role models? What type of attitude do you want future generations to embody? Are you modelling these traits and virtues, in order to help our children learn how to create a positive attitude?

A person can transform their attitude and character, each and every moment of the day. They can be mindful of their thoughts, behaviours, feelings, actions and reactions. You can decide whether you are stretching yourself and evolving as the spiritual being that you are, or whether you are choosing to stay stuck in old belief systems. The small daily stretches we make spiritually, such as deciding to embody the virtues of kindness, patience, being friendly, forgiveness and being courageous, are choices in attitude. They help a person to grow and develop spiritually. These choices help to transform an individual into the beautiful person that they were born to be. The amazing gifts that a person is given when they practice a virtue with a positive attitude, is that they will be granted peace, tranquillity, contentment and strength of character, which help sustain them in turbulent times. When you role model a positive attitude toward challenges and display all your positive character traits and virtues in the face of any difficulty that you encounter, others are inspired to do the same. When everyone around you begins to view challenges with a different attitude, we all begin to all ripple out a more positive attitude into society, which will affect more and more people around us; until many people have taken on this positive attitude and society itself begins to shift and change.

If the person chooses a positive attitude, they will start to see the virtues of others in a totally new way. You will begin to see the benefits of working with someone who has a completely opposite personality to yourself. Together your skills and strengths enable both of you to achieve so much more than if you tried to do something alone. When someone's personality traits and virtues are different from our own, we are able to see a more expanded version of the problem and the solutions, and come up with creative ways to solve problems. This win–win mentality doesn't just happen when adults work together. Adult role models are able to learn an amazing amount from children around them. Children are often much more positive than we are and they are very good at coming up with creative solutions, so we often can learn so much from children, on how to improve our attitude, perceptions, opinions of others and our attitude about life.

The very best thing we can do as role models, is to become aware of how our attitude and character impacts others and reflect on if we are impacting the children we guide in positive and inspiring ways. When we can seek to always improve our understanding of virtues, we can transform ourselves daily and choose what type of attitude we display to the world. We can choose to be more open-minded and continue to strive to make a positive difference in the world, by being a compassionate, tolerant and reflective role model, who others can look up to and choose to follow.

Every child you interact with, you have an impact on. The 9-PAC Integrity Approach Model asks that role models practice being open-minded and accepting of other people's and children's different personality styles, virtues, attitudes and beliefs, and embrace each change life brings, with a positive attitude. You can choose your attitude, because life is all about growing and becoming more than who you were a moment ago. If we can foster a strength of character within ourselves, have the ability to adapt and overcome challenges, and maintain the desire to empower others, we can truly become amazing role models to the children who look up to us. This is what it means to choose to become a 9-PAC Integrity Approach role model.

In the next chapter, we talk specifically about what type of language the 9-PAC Integrity Approach Model aims to instil in role models, so that we can all use the same empowering and uplifting style of communication, with our children. This will benefit not only the children around us, but anyone we interact with and it will positively change our society.

CHAPTER 2 – SUMMARY

- You are unique and you have gifts to offer the world that only you can

- You determine your character

- You can influence others character through role modelling

- Virtues are the ethical foundations of character

- Character traits are a set of qualities that make up a person's personality

- The Virtues Project™ helps us to understand our inherent characteristics and the virtues we have learned through our caregiver's and teacher's role modelling.

CHAPTER 3

Communication

Definition

- The act or process of using words, sounds, signs or behaviours to express or exchange information, or to express your ideas, thoughts, feelings, etc. to someone else

- A message that is given to someone: a letter, telephone call, etc.

A Pillow Full of Feathers

By Shoshannah Brombacher

In a small town somewhere in Eastern Europe, lived a nice man with a nasty problem: he talked too much about other people. He could not help himself. Whenever he heard a story about somebody he knew, and sometimes about somebody he did not know, he just had to tell it to his friends. Since he was in business, he heard quite a lot of rumours and stories. He loved the attention he got, and was delighted when they laughed because of the way he told his 'anecdotes,' which he sometimes embellished with little details he invented to make them funnier and juicier. Other than that, he was really a pleasant, good-hearted man.

He kind of knew it was wrong, but . . . it was too tempting, and in any case, most of what he told had really happened, didn't it? Many of his stories were just innocent and entertaining, weren't they?

One day he found out something really weird (but true) about another businessman in town. Of course, he felt compelled to share what he knew with his colleagues, who told it to their friends, who told it to people they knew, who told it to their wives, who spoke with their friends and their neighbours. It went around town, till the unhappy businessman who was the main character in the story heard it. He ran to the rabbi of the town, and wailed and complained that he was ruined! Nobody would like to deal with him after this. His good name and his reputation were gone with the wind.

Now this rabbi knew his customers, so to speak, and he decided to summon the man who loved to tell stories. If he was not the one who started them, he might at least know who did.

When the nice man with the nasty problem heard from the rabbi how devastated his colleague was, he felt truly sorry. He honestly had not considered it such a big deal to tell this story, because it was true; the rabbi could check it out if he wanted. The rabbi sighed.

"True, not true, that really makes no difference! You just cannot tell stories about people. This is all *lashon hara*, slander, and it's like murder—you kill a person's reputation." He said a lot more, and the man who started the rumour now felt really bad and sorry. "What can I do to make it undone?" he sobbed. "I will do anything you say!"

The rabbi looked at him. "Do you have any feather pillows in your house?" "Rabbi, I am not poor; I have a whole bunch of them. But what do you want me to do, sell them?"

"No, just bring me one."

The man was mystified, but he returned a bit later to the rabbi's study with a nice fluffy pillow under his arm. The rabbi opened the window and handed him a knife. "Cut it open!"

"But Rabbi, here in your study? It will make a mess!"

"Do as I say!"

And the man cut the pillow. A cloud of feathers came out. They landed on the chairs and on the bookcase, on the clock, on the cat which jumped after them. They floated over the table and into the teacups, on the rabbi and on the man with the knife, and a lot of them flew out of the window in a big swirling, whirling trail.

The rabbi waited ten minutes. Then he ordered the man: "Now bring me back all the feathers, and stuff them back in your pillow. All of them, mind you. Not one may be missing!"

The man stared at the rabbi in disbelief. "That is impossible, Rabbi. The ones here is the room I might get, most of them, but the ones that flew out of the window are gone. Rabbi, I can't do that, you know it!"

"Yes," said the rabbi and nodded gravely, "that is how it is: once a rumour, a gossipy story, a 'secret,' leaves your mouth, you do not know where it ends up. It flies on the wings of the wind, and you can never get it back!"

He ordered the man to deeply apologise to the person about whom he had spread the rumour; that is difficult and painful, but it was the least he could do. He ordered him to apologize to the people to whom he had told the story, making them accomplices in the nasty *lashon hara* game, and he ordered him to diligently study the laws concerning *lashon hara* every day for a year, and then come back to him.

That is what the man did. And not only did he study about *lashon hara*, he talked about the importance of guarding your tongue to all his friends and colleagues. And in the end he became a nice man who overcame a nasty problem.

Used with the permission of Shoshannah Brombacher

We educate children through how we communicate. The words we use to express our thoughts, beliefs, perceptions, our body language and our actions, are all a form of communication. Every word you speak has an energy attached to it, which is either positive or negative. You can express yourself in a way that helps to heal hearts, or in a way that causes souls to suffer. Words become our inner script and the words we use become the inner script of the children around us. When we all use a common empowering language to talk to children, we help them to build their confidence and succeed in life.

In this chapter, we will discuss the difference between language and communication and how language shows us what our character traits are and what is within our internal script. We will discuss different communication styles and a new communication style I created for the 9-PAC Integrity Approach Model, which is called the SEE-R Communication Style (Supportive, Empowering, Educational, Respectful). We will delve into how to practice mindful listening and how this can help us learn to guide children in a more compassionate way.

Most people want to create a relationship with the children in their care. However, relationships are complex and the language you use, creates the type of relationship you have with others. When you use positive, supportive and empowering language, you create positive and uplifting relationships. When you use controlling, fear-based and authoritarian language, you create relationships that are based on mistrust, anger and a lack of respect. There is a difference between communication and language. Communication is letting another person know your thoughts, needs, wants and desires, by using words and actions. Language is the tone, energy, body language and the specific type of words you use to convey your thoughts, needs, wants and desires. What is your communication style?

Communication Styles

In order for role models to communicate more effectively with children, they must become aware of their style of communicating. If we reflect on the type of communication style that we use, we can see who we learned this style from, if we want to keep it, and how we can improve upon it. This self-reflective practice, allows us to choose an effective style of communication, so that we can be effective role models, to the children that we guide.

Claire Newton, a psychologist from South Africa, states that there are five main types of communication style.

- Assertive

- Aggressive

- Passive-aggressive

- Submissive

- Manipulative

Assertive Communication Style:

The person with this type of communication style has higher self-esteem than the other styles mentioned below. They are the healthiest and most effective type of communicator. They are a true balance of aggressive, passive and assertive. When they communicate, they do not have to resort to manipulating others, to get their way. They work with people and their ideas to come up with 'win–win' solutions. The behavioural characteristics of this style is that they can achieve their goals while being aware of other's needs, have good boundaries, be respectful and they support others, while also being able to speak their needs, wants and desires. They accept and give compliments, have a positive tone of voice, open body language, use expansive hand gestures, make eye-contact and are respectful of others space. When people communicate with this person, they feel respected, they know the person will be fair, they can accept constructive criticism from them and they are more likely to try to adapt this communication style into their own inner script, because it makes them feel good about themselves. This is a style that the 9-PAC Integrity Approach Model hopes that all role models will aspire to.

The Aggressive Communication Style:

A person who communicates in this way is happy to win at someone else's expense. They want their needs met, they believe they have more rights than others and their message gets lost, because people are too busy reacting to their tone, behaviour or words, to listen to the ideas that are being illustrated. They can be frightening, loud, hostile, demanding and abrasive. Their body language is about making themselves bigger than others, they have sharp hand gestures, they frown and they get into other people's personal spaces. Their language is about put downs and insults and people on the receiving end of this communication style feel defensive, uncooperative, resentful, angry and humiliated. People do not feel heard, respected or valued with this type of communication style.

Passive-aggressive Communication Style:

In this style of communication, the person may appear to be caring and cooperative on the surface, but it actually turns out they are uncooperative. They may be acting out in anger and may be trying to get their way through sabotage, sarcasm or lying. They feel like they have a lack of power and feel resentful. They can be sarcastic, devious, patronising, sulky, and gossip about others. They do anything to get people to pay attention to them and give them energy, while pretending they are doing the opposite. They often speak in a sugary or fake tone, stand with their hand on their hip, make jerky movements, have innocent facial expressions and often touch the other person or invade their personal space. They often put their ideas down or say that no one is listening to them. People who are on the receiving end of this communication style feel confused, angry, resentful and hurt at being manipulated.

The Submissive Communication Style:

People who employ this type of communication style are worried about pleasing others and want to avoid confrontation. They act as if other's needs are more important than their own and other people have more right to contribute to the conversation, then they do. They often apologise, will not stand up for their ideas or point of view, find difficulty in making decisions and will not speak up for their needs or wants. They often blame others for the outcome of the decisions made and are often silent during group discussions. They speak with a very soft volume, make themselves seem small, do not make eye-contact and fidget. People who interact with this type of communication style feel frustrated, drained, guilty; they feel like they are taken advantage of and resent the low energy the other person gives off.

Manipulative Communication Style:

The person who uses this type of communication style is scheming to get their way and will do anything to influence others and control them into making decisions that they want made. Their message often hides their true needs and desires, but they often manage to get their way. People who use this style are controlling, ask indirectly for their needs to be met, make others feel obliged to do what they want and use artificial sulking or anger, to get what they want. They speak in patronising, envious and often high-pitched tones. They have a longing expression on their faces and people who interact with them feel guilty, frustrated, angry, resentful that they are being manipulated.

As you look over the communication styles above, reflect on when and where you have use the above styles when communicating with others and why. Which one do you use the most often? Do you use a certain style with your parents, because you feel they don't respect you and it worked as a child, to get what you want? Do you act confidently at work because you feel part of a team where everyone respects each other and is helpful to one another? Do you act aggressively around children, because it is the one place where you feel that you can be powerful?

Knowing how and why we use communication styles, is vitally important to becoming a 9-PAC Integrity Approach role model, because the style we use, deeply impacts a child's inner script. Once we know how we communicate, we can work towards building an assertive communication style, by embodying virtues that help to create this positive and empowering type of communication style. I decided to create a communication style, specifically for the 9-PAC Integrity Model.

It is called the **SEE-R Communication Style**, which is short for:

- Supportive
- Empowering
- Educational
- Respectful

The SEE-R Communication Style characteristics 'SEE', allow yourself and, potentially, the other person that you are interacting with, to feel that either one or both of you shared information that was supportive to one or both people, that one or both people were empowered by having their skills, knowledge and abilities elevated, and that what was shared, was educational, for one or both of them. The 'R' for respect, is meeting the other person at their level, where they were at in that moment, rather than where you think the other person 'should' be.

When a role model communicates to a child, colleague or any person in general they need to consider whether what they are going to say is Supportive, Empowering and Educational. Sometimes all three aspects are required, sometimes not. At the end of each conversation, the SEE-R Communication Style approach, would allow one or both parties to feel fundamentally equal and satisfied with the interaction. Both people would feel that the information shared supports them, that they felt empowered by having their skills and abilities celebrated and that either one or both individuals learned something they didn't know before. It would be a creative win–win interaction and both people would feel heard, seen and respected. When children see the SEE-R Communication Style in action, they will endeavour to imitate the role models using it, because children inherently want to help each other succeed and do what feels good for one another.

When we can switch our communication styles to embody more of the assertive characteristics and the SEE-R Communication Style method, we can consistently have positive and productive conversations with children, who will respond to us in a better way and our message will be received clearly. When we make ourselves and others feel good, we can help change the world in positive ways. A great quote to illustrate the SEE-R Communication Style concept is, "When you end a conversation, you want to leave the other people feeling happier and more empowered, than when you started the conversation."

Knowing the different types of communication styles, allows teachers, childcare educators and parents to become aware of not only how they communicate, but how the children in their care communicate. This allows them to be able to communicate much more effectively with children, if they can spot what type of communication style the child is using and help them to bring in virtues, to help them move to use the SEE-R Communication Style, on a more consistent basis. This will help children as they progress through their lives, because effective communicators can make massive change in our world, can lift others up and inspire them to also become effective communicators.

Children who have not seen these positive types of communication being used around them, may find it quite a foreign concept, to begin with, but they will feel better after each interaction and begin to model these types of communications styles, in their own lives. This will create a ripple effect and help to change social interactions around them, which will create a positive impact in the world.

The ways in which we communicate with a child impacts the rest of their life and also influences future generations. People who are emotionally strong, have positive inner scripts and want to create 'win–win' situations that bring out the best in others. Emotionally strong people empower others and help them to achieve their goals. They support them and encourage them, because they don't have any doubts, about their own self-worth and self-confidence. Effective communicators know they can get their needs met and help others meet their own needs, at the same time. They don't feel the need to compete with other people and they feel good about each interaction they have, which boosts their confidence.

We can communicate with our children on both an individual basis and a collective basis with the SEE-R Communication Style. Individually you communicate with any child in your care, through one-on-one interactions. Collectively, we communicate with children as teachers, coaches and counsellors. The more we role model the qualities of the SEE-R Communication Style on both an individual basis and collective basis, the stronger that message of empowerment will be to all children we interact with, and the faster it will be adopted into their inner scripts and cemented into their identity and subconscious.

Language

When children are born, they do not have the ability to communicate with spoken language, yet everyone is willing to 'hear' what they have to say, in whichever way they wish to express it. Children find ways to communicate to us to get their needs met, be it through crying, giggling, looking at you with soulful eyes or pulling on your clothes. The 9-PAC Integrity Approach Model believes that all role models can learn to communicate with children using a common language that is uplifting and empowering, no matter what age the child is. Our words are trusted by children, when they see that the words are backed up by our actions. This is why we need to show children that, just like them, we are growing and developing our own internal script too, and that our internal growth and development never stops during the course of our lives. We model to them, that we are always evolving and becoming better communicators.

Linda Kavelin-Popov, a co-founder of The Virtues Project™, states that "When we communicate with children and acknowledge the virtues within them, through speaking 'The Language of the Virtues', that resonates within them and they feel that they are 'seen' for who they truly are."

I remember when an acquaintance of mine, who is a counsellor, who told me about a time when she worked with challenging teenagers. She was approached to connect with a teenager who had been given her 'last opportunity' to change her negative behaviour, before she was going to be placed into the 'system'. This teenager was brought in for a session with the counsellor, who used positive language to interact with her. The counsellor said this teenager did everything she could to be disrespectful. She would not look at the counsellor, swung around her in chair, did not talk and did not appear to listen. She sat in her chair, chewing gum and tried her best to avoid any interaction with the counsellor. The counsellor was struggling to engage with her in any way and admitted to me, that she was struggling to think about the positive attributes of this teenager.

The counsellor liked to end her sessions with positive comments about the virtues that she saw in the children. She told the teenager that she could see how much determination she had, because she did everything she could, to avoid engaging in conservation with the counsellor. The teenager stopped swinging around on her chair and looked her right in the eye for the first time. The teenager later expressed, that she felt that the counsellor had seen her for who she truly was, rather than for who people thought she was. The counsellor went on to say that this girl decided that she would go to the counsellor's voluntary classes and became her biggest fan. When other troubled youth came into the voluntary class, she would tell them to listen up and pay attention to what this counsellor had to say to them.

Our words reveal our inner thoughts, beliefs and perceptions and what we think of the person we are interacting with. Words come from our inner script and showcase our personality, character traits and what virtues we embody. The words that you heard frequently spoken in childhood, as well as the energy and the tone of these words, is what you hear in your head and become your inner script. Self-talk greatly impacts your inner script, but once you become aware of what script is running in your mind, you are able to enhance or change it.

The 9-PAC model believes that speaking to children and others around us with kindness, compassion, love and guiding them through supporting their talents and skills, is an important tool, to help children, to build a positive internal script.

Having all role models speak in a consistent and empowering way to children, builds a child's self-awareness and self-confidence. When a role model frequently speaks to a child about their positive character traits, skills and virtues in encouraging ways, and when they hear that their choices have been acknowledged and supported, it allows the child to develop a positive mindset. Using positive role modelling and supportive language helps children to shift their negative character traits into positive ones. Using confidence-building language, helps children to understand their personality and virtues, and helps them to understand that they can change their thoughts, in order to change their actions. When children are able to change their thoughts, language and actions in a positive way, this creates a tolerant, supportive and peaceful environment, both for themselves and everyone around them.

When you hear someone say something negative about your skills or abilities, over a long period of time, it has a negative impact on your internal script. Children begin to criticise, judge and berate themselves, for every thought they think, every action they take and every choice they make. So often role models and children speak to themselves in a way that we would not use when we speak to our friends. We can be kind and compassionate with everyone else around us, but speak in a critical, nasty and condemning way to our own self.

Why are we so hard on ourselves? Almost everyone in the world suffers from some form of 'negative self-talk complex', at some point in their life. To improve our inner script, we need to hear positive language spoken around us, by our role models, every time they interact with us. This is how children learn to change their inner script, by seeing it role modelled and deciding to adopt this type of language and communication style. When a child begins to use positive self-talk on a daily basis, they are more likely to become successful, talented, kind, compassionate people. When people continually develop an open mindset, it leads to becoming above average achievers and having a sense of contentment within themselves.

Parents often want so much for their children that this drives them to be unnaturally hard on them. We may use language that is critical and demeaning, instead of supportive and compassionate, when we talk to our children. Our children deserve to be treated with kindness, respect and love. We must be aware that if we positively reinforce their skills and talents, if we build up their confidence and teach them self-awareness through positive language and role modelling, then we can truly help them to succeed in life.

I want to share with you a story that describes how language can affect a child's behaviour.

> Chen Miller is a special education needs teacher in Israel and, in a video recently posted to the popular Facebook page Soul Mama, she spoke about the importance of language and how we need to learn to communicate with children in positive ways. "In my first year of working in the education system, I entered a Grade 2 class room. In the centre of the room, sat a little boy with big eyes. He cursed, spat, and screamed. He looked at me and I looked at him. I went closer and whispered to him, "I know you have a big heart. I know that you're clever, I know that you're a good boy." In front of the whole class, he said, "Stupid teacher, you don't know anything. I'm a disturbed boy. Everyone knows I am disturbed. The teachers say I'm disturbed, the headmaster says I'm disturbed. Even my parents say I'm disturbed."

> "You have a big heart, you are a clever boy and I know you're a good boy." I said. The little boy ran out the class.

> The second week, when I entered the class, it was the same script. Cursing, screaming, spitting. I took a deep breath, went close to him and whispered, "I know you have a big heart. I know that you're clever, I know that you're a good boy."

> The third week when I entered the class, a little seat was waiting next to my own seat, and on that little seat, sat a little boy with big eyes. That day he chose me to be his teacher.

Towards the end of the year he asked me how did I know that children are good? I told him that I had a secret. Until fifth grade, I didn't know how to read or write and I couldn't connect numbers together. I thought I was stupid, I thought I had a broken brain and I was sure that nothing good would come out of me.

I, Chen Miller, the student of a special needs' class, became a teacher in Israel. Me, the one the system was going to give up on, more than once.

I am now in the system to change it, to show that it can be done differently. Teachers, headmasters, educators . . . your thoughts and the words that you use about a child will at some stage become the thoughts and words the child thinks about themselves. "I won't succeed. Nothing good will become of me; I am incapable, I'm lazy, I can't".

There is no child that can't; only a child that can! Remember always, that education is forming of impressions on souls."[1]

In this example, the language used by the teacher was positive, empowering, and was a language from the heart. It helped her get through to the student, who up to that point, had only been spoken to in detrimental ways. He had virtually no positive role models in his life. This example show us that just one positive role model can make a huge impact in the life of a child and that is why I wrote this book, *How to Raise Children with Integrity*, to help all role models learn to become the very best communicators they can be, so that they too can be the person, that will make a difference in the lives of the children around them. When role models all use an engaging, empowering, supportive and compassionate common language, it reaches children at their heart level and over time, can help heal

---

[1] This Israeli Teacher has a powerful message for kids with special needs.

the wounds created by unaware role models and they can begin to choose a new inner script; which will help them succeed in life.

This is why the 9-PAC Integrity Approach Model is so crucial to begin using right away. When we can become better role models to our children, speak in empowering ways to our families, our communities and the people around us in society, we become the change that we want to see in the world. The more people who speak the same empowering language, the more children it will help and they will adopt it and start to lift up the children around them. This is how role models are formed. A role model is not just an adult, it can be children role modelling for each other.

Words truly do have the power to change the world. Can you imagine the difference it would have made to your life, if every word that was spoken to you was positive? If every word that was spoken to you empowered you to discover who you were meant to be and inspired you to follow your dreams and live the life you yearned to live? I cannot emphasize strongly enough how crucial it is to speak lovingly and kindly to our future citizens, in order to help them create the future that they are worthy and capable of creating. The language they use will create their inner script, which will affect all of us in the long run and will also affect their children and how they make choices in the world.

Mindful Listening

Have you ever heard the expression, "We have two eyes, two ears and one mouth?" This phrase means that we were designed to watch and listen twice as much, as we were to speak. 'Listen' and 'silent' have the same letters in them. When we listen, we learn. When we talk, we do not learn anything, but rather speak our needs, desires, thoughts, and opinions, to the other person. We are stating what we already know and what we want to get from others. We are trying to sway people to believe, what we believe or get them to agree, with something we said.

Mindful listening means being fully present in each moment, with kindness and without judgment. Jon Kabat-Zinn states in his 1994 book, *Wherever You Go, There You Are*, that mindful listening is "Paying attention in a particular way, on purpose, in the present moment and non-judgmentally." Mindful listening encourages you to let go of distractions and your physical and emotional reactions, to what people say to you. When you are mindful, you are not distracted by your own thoughts and worries, the emotional responses your body makes to the words that a person says, or the opinions that they speak. When you plan your response to the person's comment, while you should be listening to them, you are not able to become aware of their communication style, choice of words, their intended message and what they are requiring from you.

Good Listeners

Real listeners are open-minded and are genuinely interested in what the other person has to say, no matter if it matches their beliefs or not. They allow the other person the time and space to fully say what they need to say and look deeper than the surface meaning. They seek to understand where the speaker is 'coming from' and what purpose, interest or need, could be motivating the conversation. Good listening encourages others to feel heard, understood and respected.

Poor Listeners

Poor listeners or underdeveloped listeners, are unable to separate their own needs, desires and interests from those of the person who is speaking. They are constantly asking themselves, "How does this affect me and what can I say next, in order to get my way?" Poor listeners often interrupt, finish the other person's sentences and ignore things that are of no interest to them. They do not seek what is 'between the lines' or notice what the other person is saying with their body language and communication style. When they speak, they are typically telling the other person their own opinions or to debate what was said, so that they can assert their dominance over the conversation.

Deep Listening

Deep listening involves listening on a deeply receptive, empathic and compassionate level. A deep listener puts themselves in the other person's shoes, attempts to see things from their perspective and attempts to understand the other person's inner script, so they can determine what is driving the reason for the conversation. Is the other person looking for sympathy, support, or kindness? Are they just excited and want to share that with others? Or are they looking for more, in terms of asking for money or time? Deep listeners think about what the other person is saying, before they respond. They ask for clarification on what was said, by retelling the highlights of the story and asking if they received the message properly. Their listening style is generous, empathic, supportive, accurate, and trusting. Trust does not imply agreement, trust in this sense means that no matter what was said, or how it came across, that the person respected what the other person said, honoured and processed it at a deep level. Deep Listening suspends self-oriented, reactive thinking and opens a person up to a greater level of awareness, so they can absorb new and unexpected ways of thinking and alternate kinds of information.

Becoming an Effective Listener

It can be hard to be a good listener or a deep listener, because people's words or phrases can create an emotional reaction, in our body. We might feel a 'knot' in our stomach, a 'lump' in our throat, or feel 'emotionally charged', by the things people say to us. These body reactions can trigger strong emotions and emotional responses, which can in turn, can hamper our ability to listen effectively. A good listener and a deep listener would pause, breathe, let the emotions come up for them, acknowledge them, but keep listening to the other person; knowing that they are not in any specific danger from the person's words, even though their body may be telling them that. If we as listeners can notice these slight inner sensations, before they take over our mental capacity, we can stop ourselves from being overwhelmed by the other person's words and continue listening, instead of reacting.

For example, suppose that a child in your classroom has come to tell you about a time when they were mistreated by their parents. Our first thoughts might be anger, fear or judgment against the parents and a need for retribution. We may want to immediately call the police and may want to hold the child and protect them. A good listener would allow these emotions to come up and acknowledge them, but continue to be respectful of what the child was saying and what they wanted out of the conversation. A good listener would be aware enough to ask gentle questions to clarify what they think happened and ask the child how they feel about the mistreatment in supportive ways. They can acknowledge how hard it would be for the child to tell them this information and that they are there to help the child feel safe and supported. The child will feel heard, seen, respected and not imposed upon or pressured. In this type of environment, a proper and appropriate solution, can be found.

Teachers and parents can talk to children about mindful listening and explain how to become a mindful listener. A teacher could set up a time, perhaps daily or weekly, to tell the students a story or explain an idea to them and then give them the opportunity to individually explain what they thought the teacher was trying to convey; either in a group setting or on paper. The students could explain what they thought the teacher wanted from them, the ideas, needs and desires that the teacher wanted the listener to hear and what the deeper meaning of the story was. They can explain which communication style they believed the teacher was using, what type of language the teacher displayed and what their character and personality traits might be. The children can then take time to write out or think about what their response would be to the person, taking into consideration the virtues of empathy, compassion, tolerance, while being objective and trying to create a supportive win–win solution.

Mindful listening is something that will take time to learn, but it does not need to be difficult. It is about learning how to respond, instead of reacting. To become a mindful listener requires a person to be present, to be in the moment and not let things distract them; such as their surroundings, their electronics, or their worries or fears. Mindful listening allows a role model to see and understand the true character of a child, identify their strengths, weaknesses, inner script and the communication style they use most often. This can help a role model to support and celebrate the virtues and skills that are unique to the child and help them move towards using the SEE-R Communication style, which helps them to cultivate the ability, to listen mindfully.

Pausing before speaking is the key to mindful listening, because it illustrates that you are considering what has been said and are digesting the information. It serves to slow down the process of communication, which can inject a sense of space and calm into a conversation that may be emotionally charged. This provides a space for the speaker to talk and to pause. It can allow the speaker to collect their thoughts, expand on something or clarify what they said, in a better way. When we jump in and react, we can disrupt the flow of communication. Pauses and silence are beneficial when communicating as pauses provide time for processing and reflecting on what has been said and provides an opportunity to respond rather than reaction. This is practice I strongly encourage when communicating, especially in situations that have emotional charge as words that are said cannot be unsaid. I call these momentary reflections.

Mindful listening is the spirit of non-defensiveness and is the attitude of attempting to understand and acknowledge another's feelings and point of view. When we as 9-PAC Integrity Approach role models listen to children and others around us in this way, we create a loving and supportive environment, where everyone feels heard, appreciated and respected. Thoughts create behaviours and when we feel safe, we behave in less aggressive ways. When parents, teachers and childcare educator, practice this type of listening in their homes, communities and in the classroom, they create a climate of honesty, respect and trust. People can get more accomplished, because everyone learns to adopt this type of listening style and people feel safe to express their wants, needs, desires and ideas. Everyone's ideas are acknowledged and thought about in terms of win–win solutions and everyone wants to help each other to grow and succeed.

The children will take this new listening style and incorporate it into their inner script, because it makes them feel good to practice it. Once it becomes a subconscious behaviour, they will carry on using it their entire lives and role model it to everyone around them, who will also enjoy the benefits of mindful listening and a ripple will again happen; creating the change we want to see in the world and our society. If many children grew up to use this type of listening style, our very society would look vastly different than it does now and the world would be a much better place to live in.

The barriers to mindful listening are allowing ourselves to get put on autopilot by social media, video games and our electronics. A barrier can also be our ego, which only wants to focus on itself and its needs. The third barrier is our intolerances for other's viewpoints and opinions, which may be different than our own. The final thing that can create a barrier to mindful listening, is our own negative self-talk and wounded inner script. This can distract a person from what the other person is saying, colour what they say with the listeners own hurts and fears and prevent them from fully hearing what is being conveyed by the speaker.

The way to break down these barriers, is to be aware of which ones you personally face, and work towards overcoming them by picking virtues that will help you to become a more mindful listener, and work on being a mindful listener in each of your interactions, with other people and children. You can pause before you speak, so you can consider the effect of your words on others, pay attention to the deeper messages in people's words, and work to become more aware and tolerant of the differences between your thoughts and ideas and the person's thoughts and ideas.

By mindfully using positive language in your communication style, you will now be able to recognise when you are expressing yourself in a manner that is supportive, empowering and respectful to the children you guide. You will be able to become a mindful listener and create an environment where the child feels seen, heard and respected. When all role models adopt the 9-PAC Integrity Approach Model of empowering language and SEE-R Communication, we strive to help children heal the wounds to their inner script and help them to choose the traits and virtues that will enable them to become amazing role models and future leaders. When we talk from the heart and use positive and supportive language, we help to grow their confidence and self-esteem, so that they are better able to create win–win conversations with people who they interact. They will be able to think, act and listen in mindful and compassionate ways, which help to create engaging and constructive dialogues with others; where both people's needs are met and both parties understand what the other person is wanting. These children will grow into amazing adults, who are able to shift our societal norms and values around communication, from a self-centred society, to a society that focuses on togetherness, empathy and compassion. Imagine the impact it would have on the workforce in future generations if child were taught, and continued to speak, to each other using the SEE-R communication method?

Lastly, the THINK Method is important for role models to remember when communicating to our children. Before you speak is it:

T – is it True?

H – is it Helpful

I – is it Inspiring?

N – is it Necessary?

K – is it Kind?

In the next chapter, we will talk about choices and how small choices can have big impacts, on every part of our lives. I will discuss how we can help children learn to consistently make positive and uplifting choices, throughout their lives.

CHAPTER 3 – SUMMARY:

- Words can hurt and crush a spirit. Words can become someone else's inner voice

- Language creates our internal script and the internal script of children

- What is your communication style? What is the child's communication style that you are interacting with?

- Role modelling is the strongest method of communicating our thoughts and beliefs

- Use the SEE-R Communication Method:
  S – Supportive
  E – Empowering
  E – Education
  R – Respectful – meet them where they are at right now

- How to engage in Mindful Listening

SECTION 2

Choices, Consequences, Culture

All choices have consequences
which create our culture

CHAPTER 4

Choices

Definition

- The act of choosing: the act of picking or deciding between two or more possibilities

- The opportunity or power to choose between two or more possibilities: the opportunity or power to make a decision

- A range of things that can be chosen

"Take the first step in faith. You don't have to see the whole staircase, just take the first step."

Dr Martin Luther King Jr

The Story of Two Wolves

Native American — A Cherokee legend that illustrates our choice between good and bad.

An old Cherokee is teaching his grandson about life. "A fight is going on inside me," he said to the boy.

"It is a terrible fight and it is between two wolves.

"One is evil — he is anger, envy, sorrow, regret, greed, arrogance, self-pity, guilt, resentment, inferiority, lies, false pride, superiority and ego."

He continued "The other is good — he is joy, peace, love, hope, serenity, humility, kindness, benevolence, empathy, generosity, truth, compassion and faith.

"The same fight is going on inside you — and inside every other person too."

The grandson thought about it for a minute and then asked his grandfather "Which wolf will win?"

The old Cherokee simply replied, "The one you feed".

Children learn their entire decision-making system from watching their parents, caregivers and teachers make decisions, face consequences and accept mistakes. The actions that we display and the choices we make are preparing children to learn to make their own decisions, hopefully with wisdom, reflection, compassion and awareness. Learning from our mistakes and becoming an objective decision maker, will help future generations, make decisions based on the greater good and 'win–win' outcomes; instead of making decisions from reaction-based models.

In this chapter, we will discuss how to teach a child to use the 9-PAC Integrity Approach Mode decision making system. In this system, a role model helps children to understand their choices, by assisting them to consider the potential consequences of each choice they could make. This will not only build their confidence, but also broaden their mindset to think beyond conditioned patterns and beliefs. The system teaches children how to research their choices, reflect on how their choices will affect others, use forward planning, and understand, how small choices can create big impacts in the world around them. I will also discuss how role model's mistakes can be used as teaching lessons, to help children become more objective and compassionate decision makers. The model also teaches children about appropriate limits, how their personality affects their decision-making abilities and how their self-talk can help or hinder them when making decisions.

It is possible to teach a child of any age how to use the 9-PAC Integrity Approach decision-making model, by offering choices to them. This allows them to feel as if they are contributing to how the family or classroom operates and gives them a sense of control over their own life. For example, if a parent asked a child if they would like a bath before or after dinner, it empowers them to make a reflective decision and when the parent explains the consequences of either choice, the child can then make an informed decision on what works best for them and for the family. In this example, the parent is not giving the child a choice on whether to have a bath or not, they are asking the child when they would like to have a bath, based on a set of choices that were considered by the parent, prior to the discussion. This allows for a 'win–win' situation. The child feels like they have control over their life, they learnt how to make a choice based on two options and two potential consequences and they made a choice that the family was already happy with; which made everyone feel good. This allowed them to learn to be reflective and learn a positive decision-making strategy, in a safe and supportive environment.

Learning this decision-making model very early in a child's life can help them tremendously in every aspect of their early years and moving forward into the school system, as well as later on in their work careers. It also helps them to build strong relationships in their families and communities. The family unit functions better when parents and children make informed and compassionate choices that work towards creating a family unit, that is functional and respectful. The classroom, community or culture arena is no different as the 9-PAC model supports quality teaching in a positive learning environment regardless of whether the child is at home, school or in another community setting. When individuals make decisions based on the 9-PAC Integrity Approach Model, they make informed and positive decisions that take into account everyone's ideas and needs due to the open-mindedness learning, which allows for empowered choices to be made and implemented. It creates situations where there are no surprise consequences that arise, or harsh backlash from decision-making members who felt that they never were heard or respected.

People in Positions of Power

Children often look up to people in positions of power and try to emulate them. When a child sees their parents, teachers and community members following or admiring the character traits of a celebrity, sportsperson or political leader, they begin to emulate this behaviour as well, so that they will fit into their community and family culture more easily. When children see their role model's approving of a person in powers behaviour, they believe it must be the correct way to behave, even if the behaviour is negative. When people in positions of power behave deploringly, rebel against the law, and/or take drugs, children will also emulate these behaviours. Who we admire as role models affects who our children emulate, which in turn affects their behaviour. Therefore, it is essential for role models to be aware of whom they admire and consider whether this person is a good example for the children that they guide and parent, to be exposed to.

The everyday words and actions of regular adults in positions of power, such as a doctor, nurse, police officer, teacher, religious leader or coach, can impact our children's developing viewpoints and has a significant impact on their inner script. From a child's perspective, whether the behaviour and attitude displayed towards the child is caring and supportive or power hungry and controlling, will affect their inner beliefs and self-confidence. That is why every adult is considered to be a role model, as children are always watching and mimicking our character traits, behaviours, perspectives, words and choices. For example, a child who comes into contact with a gruff police officer, a distracted and distant doctor or an authoritarian teacher, may form the opinion that people in power need to act gruff, aloof and behave in authoritarian ways. They see their caregivers approving of these people's behaviour and so they begin to act in the same way, because they think that this is how people in positions of power should behave.

A parent or role model, can explain to a child why they admire someone. They can discuss what they like about the person's personality and character traits, the decisions the person made that they agreed with, and why they admire the person. A role model can explain to a child why they wish to emulate the person's behaviour and how they are going to copy the person's positive virtues, so they can change their own inner script and become more like the person they admire.

It is important to help children understand that everyone has their own issues and inner scripts, and that everyone has had different role models in their lives. This assists the child in understanding that they need to reflect on the behaviour of people in power, and judge for themselves if it was appropriate. They can also consider if the person in power could have acted in a better way or have made better choices. Role models can show children that adults make many different choices in life, face the consequences of those choices, make mistakes and always have room to improve their character. Role models can explain that one bad decision does not mean that a person is a bad person for the rest of their life and that everyone can change their inner script to become the person they wish to be.

For example, a teacher could carry out an exercise in class, in which children are asked who they admire and why. They could list what they like about this role model and how the role model has affected their life; their personality, character traits, decisions and inner script. The children could then reflect on whether they think the role model is a good choice or not, and why. Following this, the children could then decide if they want to copy this person's character traits and behaviours, in their own lives. This allows the children to think mindfully about all role models in their life and to consciously choose whether they want to copy that behaviour or not, instead of blindly following someone or emulating their behaviours simply because their parents or friends do. Educating our children to become independent thinkers is one of the most powerful gifts we can give them.

Making mindful decisions is a behaviour that the 9-PAC Integrity Approach Model hopes that all parents, teachers, childcare educators and children will learn to practice in their lives. Every person sees a role model differently and values their skills, talents, behaviours and the choices they make, in unique ways. Not every role model will resonate with each person or child, in the same way and that is quite acceptable. We all need to find role models that resonate with us, but also be mindful as to why that person resonates with us. For example, we might like a movie star who is tough and courageous, because these are character traits that we would like to embody in our own life. However, not every part of the person's personality or choices, are something that we want to emulate. This is why it is important to be mindful of which aspects of the role model's behaviours you want to integrate into your own life and which parts you don't want to copy.

Making Self-Aware Choices

Teaching a child about their virtues or character traits, how they feel when they practice a particular virtue, and how they feel when someone else practices a virtue, empowers them to become a reflective and mindful individual. It enables them to consider the bigger picture of what is going on around them and why the person may have reacted or chose to behave, in the way that they did. When an individual can recognise virtues in themselves and others, as well as recognise and verbally express when they believe that people are not displaying positive characteristics and virtues – they are learning to be reflective of the inner traits of people around them. People often damage themselves and others around them by acting in an unaware fashion. When individuals can begin to make choices based on self-awareness and choose to not only help themselves, but the community and world around them, our world will become a better place.

In order to make self-aware choices, a person needs to be self-aware. Not only considering the bigger picture, but understanding the consequences of their decisions and how the consequences will affect others around them and society. Self-awareness is looking beyond a person's own self, their own ideas, beliefs and perceptions, and looking at the world from an objective viewpoint. This allows an individual to see the big picture much more easily and to make decisions and act in ways that help to enhance their community, society and the world.

The goal of the 9-PAC Integrity Approach Model, is to help all role models to learn to think, act and behave in self-aware ways, so that they can help to make the world a better place for our future generations. When role models help children learn to incorporate these decision-making tools into their inner script, they can help guide children to use these processes to help our society, continue to evolve in the future, and help to create a better world, for generations to come. Children who learn to internalise these 9-PAC decision-making processes, become the future role models for the children in their care and these positive decision-making systems continue to be practiced, until they become normalised into society.

For example, a teacher with an older class, could discuss a world event and which decisions had negative or positive consequences for a community or country. The students can view the event as a case study exercise. They can look at who made the decisions, was it a single person or a group, and whether it was made from an unaware or aware mindset. They can then examine which character traits may have caused the mindset used by the decision makers and discuss what type of inner script they think the decision makers had. The students could discuss if the decision makers behaved in supportive and understanding ways, if everyone understood the choices and consequences, and if was everyone's opinion was taken into account.

Following this, the class could discuss how the decision-making process could have been conducted in a better way. The students could map out their own process, see if the same choices and consequences would be considered and determine if they would make a similar or different decision. They could then look at the possible outcomes from the decisions that they chose to make. This exercise could also be carried out by teachers or parents with younger children, using a storybook character that made a decision as the case study, then follow the same reflective process to teach them how to make self-aware decisions.

Assisting a child to reflect on the decisions placed before them, shows them how to consider the ways that their thoughts impact their actions, as well as how their behaviour impacts other people in their lives. As children face difficulties in their lives, make choices and face consequences, it is important that they have a solid, aware and compassionate decision-making foundation. When a child can reflect internally and externally, on the choices they are face and see the potential consequences of their choices before they make them, they can begin to act in ways that strengthen their relationships, enhance their communities and help society evolve into a utopian paradigm.

Teaching Limits

Everything in life requires balance and moderation. It is important that we understand how this balance affects, the choices we make, how we behave and interact with others, and how it affects our inner script. There are some choices that children are not yet capable of making, such as leading a family unit, although there are some parents who allow their children to run the household, through giving into their child's temper tantrums.

Some parents may feel too tired to take a particular action or make a certain decision, however choosing 'not to decide' *is* in fact deciding. It is choosing to leave the decision up to others to decide for you, rather than taking control of your life and what happens around you. Every moment of life is about making decisions and choices. "Will I set the alarm so that I have time to go for a walk before breakfast? Which virtue do I need to focus on today? What tasks do

I have to do today?" Every day is about learning and growing into the person you want to be in life.

Some parents give their power away by 'giving in' to their child and letting them control the direction of each day and each event. The parent is making a choice, not to positively role model cooperation strategies and decision-making skills to their child. This behaviour on the parent's part, might be because of the script they adopted from watching their caregivers in early childhood, or because they felt they had no control over their own life when they were younger and do not want their child to feel that way as well. Regardless of the motivation this behaviour is not reflective or self-aware. No matter what your inner script is at this moment, you can always begin to change it, so that you can become a better role model for the children in your life and make decisions that help to teach your children how to become better leaders in our world. Children who learn to be child tyrants act the same way when they grow up.

If we wish to change the direction of society, we need to help the children around us, learn to have more positive inner scripts and to have better decision-making abilities. We also need to teach children how to become self-aware and self-reflective, so that they can see how their choices, behaviours and beliefs, affect the people around them, their community and society. When children become better role models, they become more compassionate teachers, politicians, lawyers, doctors and future citizens.

A child also needs to learn that some things have distinct limits. As children grow, they constantly learn and test boundaries and learn what happens when they make decisions. Limits help them to become aware, of what is appropriate and what is not appropriate. While assisting children to make choices, we need to be aware of our role as an adult and their role as a child. For example, a child may want to go for a bike ride, but is unaware of how this decision will impact their family. Perhaps their sister has a swimming lesson or one of the parents may have an appointment to get to. If the child is unaware of their limits, the family's plans and what needs to happen during the day, their decision will be based on a lack of knowledge and a lack of awareness, which will create consequences that neither the child, nor the family will like. The child will get into trouble for not being aware of the family's needs and plans, leading everyone to feel upset and frustrated with each other. The best way to teach children to be self-aware, is to teach them to first gather all the information they need, in order to make their decision.

Either a child, a parent, childcare educator or teacher could learn, and teach, how to be considerate. By asking others what they need help with in order to ensure that an individuals', family or school activities are completed so everyone benefits from having quality time together. A child could learn to be considerate by asking what the family plans are for the day so they are aware of what time they need to have themselves and their things ready for if there are any activities organised. They can then consider this information then decide how to fit in the family arrangements with their plans. They could then take several options to their parents and ask them for their feedback. They could propose that they would like to take a bike ride, if there is time before the family must leave for an appointment and suggest that they wear a watch to ensure that they will return ten minutes before they time, that everyone has to leave. They could also propose that they ride their bike in the front or back of the house, until everyone is ready to leave. Alternatively, they could play a game, because there is not time for a bike ride, but request that the parents make time later on, for the child to be allowed to go for a longer bike ride. All of these options show awareness of not only what the child wants, but shows respect for the family's plans and their needs as well.

When a parent listens to the child's option, they could let the child know which one works best for the family and for them and what the potential consequences are, of each choice. The child could then choose what they want to do, having made a fully informed decision and with knowledge of the consequences of their choices and actions. If the child chooses to go for the bike ride, but does not come back on time and disrupts the family's plans, then they would be aware of the consequence they would face which may be not being allowed to go on bike rides prior to family outings in future. This process creates awareness for the entire family and everyone knows what is going on and why decisions are being made.

Often parents and teachers are very good at giving directions, but not very good at giving all the information or reasons behind why they make a decision. This creates a society of followers, who are not self-reflective and are unaware of how to make informed decisions. It is ironic how we as a society get flustered when young individuals do not know how to make proper decisions, and we wonder why this is the case. If we want to teach children how to make informed and aware decisions, that follow an objective decision-making process, we must teach them how to do this and guide them through the process in supportive and compassionate ways. We also need to allow them to make mistakes and learn from their mistakes. Children have different processing capacities than adults, less life experience and have made fewer mistakes, from which to draw wisdom from when making decisions. If we teach children properly about how to make informed decisions, we are helping them to become amazing decision makers throughout their lives, and the consequences they create will be much more appropriate and acceptable to our society; because they will be based on mindfulness and self-awareness.

Limits help everyone to know what is acceptable and not acceptable in society. If children are unaware of their limits, valuable information is withheld from their decision-making processes. If a child does not know what the rules are, how can they follow them? Also, a child may know the rules, but not understand why they are in place or what consequences can happen, when a rule is not followed. For example, adults often tell children not to take drugs, but we don't tell them why, other than "It will hurt you". Adults often do not provide enough information on the consequences of taking drugs. The effect of drugs on the body, mind and the people around them, should be explained. The role model could explain the impact that taking drugs could have on their future, short-term and long-term consequences. Role models could explain that the long-term affect could be that many people become addicted and it leads to a life where nothing else matters, except getting access to the drugs and the things they do in order to obtain the drugs. They can explain how drugs impact on a person physically, emotionally and spiritually and how it negatively impacts on their relationships with the people around them, and especially their children. If the children have this information, they will be able to make informed, self-aware decisions. Knowledge is powerful and helps people to make appropriate decisions that take others into account. When role models fail to provide children with all of the information they need, children subsequently make poor decisions. The fault lies not with the child's processes, but our own processes.

The 9-PAC Integrity Approach Model, teaches children not only how to become better decision makers, but also teaches their role model how to become more aware and reflective, of the information they give out. Everyone needs to receive enough information, in order to make proper decisions. Often children will bring up points we miss, because they see the world from a much different perspective than we do. Adults can be less objective because of old belief systems and often have the habit of making assumptions. Adults can learn as much from children, as children can learn from adults and we should be open to their questions and ideas, to help ourselves grow and evolve. The 9-PAC Integrity Approach Model, believes that everyone is equal and that all points of view are valuable. This consideration of each person and their thoughts, allows society to keep evolving, so that we can create a world of tolerance, wisdom, compassion and reflection. When all points of view are considered and our choices are based on how our actions will affect others, as well as, taking into account our own wants and needs, we embody the virtues of integrity, objectivity and awareness cultivating a society that is run by reflective and conscientious adults.

Personality, Balance and Mistakes

When guiding children in the decision-making process, we can ask them what feels right; not just for them, but for everyone else involved. Some personalities will put others first and forget to take care of themselves, which can lead to a life-long struggle of giving away their own power. Other personalities have no issue putting themselves above everyone else and will do whatever it takes to get what they want, regardless of who or what is in their way or the emotional damage that they may inflict upon others and themselves.

Once a child is aware of the balance they must strive for, based on their personality, characteristic traits and inner script, they then need to know all the potential options available to them and the consequences of those choices. Once they have this information, a parent or teacher can then ask the child to share their thoughts on all these possibilities and what feels right for them. Guiding the child to understand each choice, how it works or does not work for them, and how it affects those around them. They can then let the child make a choice and support them in that choice. Not all children will make appropriate choices, and this is when the role model will need to explain to the child the reason that choice may not have been the best choice for them to make. There will be times when you, as a role model, will not be comfortable with a child's choice. However, in most circumstances, unless their choice will have drastic consequences for them or others, it is best to support them in their choice and allow them to learn through trial and error and accepting the known, and sometimes unknown consequences.

As adults, we can look back and know that often we had to make mistakes ourselves, in order to learn from them. Only hearing what a consequence might be was not enough for us to just make the appropriate choice, we had to try it out for ourselves. Mistakes, and accepting consequences that comes from those mistakes, are important things for children to learn to accept and navigate in their lives. If we deprive them of these crucial life skills, we are only enabling a future generation that will not have proper decision-making skills and will not accept ownership of their own choices. When children are aware that they have the capability to make a decision and that they have your support, it teaches them that life provides many experiences and that you believe in them, no matter what choice they make. This supports them to grow and expand, make decisions and fail, in a caring and reflective environment.

Our own mistakes can become learning forums for children, as they are able to see that adults make mistakes too, but can learn from them and make better choices going forward. If children can see role models evolving before their very eyes, it allows them to understand that they too can evolve and become better people. For example, a child may have made an unfortunate mistake in the past and they now believe they are not a good person because of it. They continually act in detrimental ways and make poor decisions, because they believe they are bad and cannot change. However, if a child can see a teacher, parent or childcare educator make a mistake and then learn from it, they can understand that one bad decision does not create a lifelong pattern of behaviour, and that people can change their behaviour and thoughts, at any time.

When role models react to difficult events and display strength of character and integrity, they model to children a positive decision-making system that children can internalise and model. When role models admire people who help society, who believe in the collective good and who act in reflective and thoughtful ways, children learn to also model these examples of resilience, service to others and how to engage in responsible behaviour. They become role models who are admired and emulated, and the positive pattern continues to ripple out into society and create a worldwide movement of empowerment and support for everyone. When children learn how to make decisions, see potential consequences, reflect on how it will affect others and accept the mistakes they make, they will become decision makers that can make positive and lasting change in our world. Change comes from within each of us and how we role model decision making processes to the children in our lives. We *can* be the change we want to see in the world and we *can* become the difference makers; by helping to guide children in the 9-PAC Integrity Approach Model system.

CHAPTER 4 – SUMMARY

- Choosing not to decide is choosing to decide

- Always offer acceptable choices and explain the consequences. Always support the child's choice

- Admit to your mistakes and use them to show children how to make more appropriate decisions

- Teach children limits, respect, balance and to make self-aware choices

- Your past does not determine your future; anyone can change their inner script and change their behaviour

- The 9-PAC decision-making system and how to explain this to children: choices, consequences and considering other's feelings, wants and needs

CHAPTER 5

Consequences

Definition

- Something that happens as a result of a particular action or set of conditions

- Importance or value

"If humanity does not

opt for integrity,

we are through completely.

It is absolutely touch and go.

Each one of us

could make the difference."

R. Buckminster Fuller

Children Learn What They Live

By Dorothy Law Nolte, Ph.D.

If children live with criticism, they learn to condemn.

If children live with hostility, they learn to fight.

If children live with fear, they learn to be apprehensive.

If children live with pity, they learn to feel sorry for themselves.

If children live with ridicule, they learn to feel shy.

If children live with jealousy, they learn to feel envy.

If children live with shame, they learn to feel guilty.

If children live with encouragement, they learn confidence.

If children live with tolerance, they learn patience.

If children live with praise, they learn appreciation.

If children live with acceptance, they learn to love.

If children live with approval, they learn to like themselves.

If children live with recognition, they learn it is good to have a goal.

If children live with sharing, they learn generosity.

If children live with honesty, they learn truthfulness.

If children live with fairness, they learn justice.

If children live with kindness and consideration, they learn respect.

If children live with security, they learn to have faith in themselves and in those about them.

If children live with friendliness, they learn the world is a nice place in which to live.

Every action has a reaction, which is either positive or negative. Sometimes these consequences may appear negative, but in the long term, an individual realises they were positive events, that were character building opportunities. These consequences made the person stronger emotionally, intellectually and spiritually. Unfortunately, there are no crystal balls that are able to foresee exactly how consequences will play out in our lives or in society. From the decisions that people make, or exactly what actions are best taken to move forward and for humanity to progress and advance. The best anyone can do, is to being able to look at situations from different perspectives, consider potential outcomes and make decisions with as much information as individuals are able to obtain.

Taking responsibility for our decisions and the consequences that come from them is empowering and helps to remove a person's defensiveness around the idea that they have to make perfect decisions every time and always make the 'right' decision. Many people have an inner script assumption, that they cannot make a mistake when they are acting as a role model. The 9-PAC Integrity Approach role model knows that making mistakes are part of life and that these mistakes can be used as teaching case studies, for the children that they guide. Mistakes open a person up to pleasant surprises that they had not anticipated, in the form of learning opportunities, character building gifts and the ability to be reflective on their inner script and personality. Mistakes allow us to grow and become better in every aspect of our inner and outer lives.

In this chapter I will discuss if choices are conscious or unconscious, how to anticipate the consequences to decisions that we are considering and how to help children learn to be mindful of the possible consequences. I will discuss how to take full responsibility for the decisions you make as a role model and how to help children take responsibility for their choices and the consequences of such choices. Even though consequences can be uncomfortable, they can teach children valuable life lessons. Consequences help us all become more aware and mindful in our decision-making processes.

Conscious or Unconscious?

Are the consequences to your decisions Conscious or Unconscious? Consequences can be unconscious if we have not reflected on the impact that they will have in our lives or the lives of the people around us. They can also be unconscious, because of a lack of information on what consequences may occur after we have made our decision. For example, if we are working on a creative project that no one in our circle or community has attempted before, we will not necessarily know what the consequences of our decisions may be.

We can research possible outcomes, but we would be making a guess, as to what may happen, but will not know with any certainty what the outcome of our decision will be.

Conscious decisions occur when we reflect on the possible decisions we can make, gather information on the possible or known consequences, determine how it will affect us and others around us, and we choose to make a decision based off of all this information. The 9-PAC Integrity Approach Model teaches that all role models should be aware of what their perceptions are, and what their values, beliefs and personal experiences are, when considering what decision to make. This creates a decision-making process that stops being emotionally charged and reaction based decisions from being made. This allows for a more rational and well thought out, objective decision-making process to occur. It also allows for consequences to be known, so the individual can pick the best option, not only for them, but for those around them in a 'win–win' approach to decision making.

When an individual reflects on whether a decision has a conscious or unconscious consequence, they are able to decide if they need to gather more information on the subject, to see what types of consequences may occur; the likelihood of them occurring and if there are any unknown consequences that they might not be aware of. It is often the unknown consequences that impact others and the individual the most and create regrets and far reaching consequences in their communities and society. For example, when engineers built buildings on an old earthquake fault, but were unaware of the fault or the consequences of building structures that did not meet earthquake codes, and eventually disaster struck and the buildings collapsed. The people who made the decision to build, did not reflect on all the information they needed to be aware of and the possible consequences of their actions. Our society is riddled with these types of decisions that are made every day by people who made decisions based on ego, greed, emotion and ignorance. Raising kids with integrity, is attempting to halt the flow of these type of reactionary decision-making strategies and create a new more reflective 9-PAC strategy. Which takes into account as many factors objectively as possible from many different people's perspectives. It takes into account the wellbeing of all people, creatures and the environment and hopes to guide a generation of role models to help their children and the children they guide, to become better decision makers, in our lifetime.

As role models, our decision-making abilities are seen by the children around us, at every moment. What type of decision-making strategy do you employ? Aware and reflective or emotional and reaction based? How do you make decisions when stressed or frustrated? Our character traits and virtues come out strongly, in times of stress, and that is when we are able to see, what our inner script decision making style is. When we reflect on our past decisions, we are able to see what type of style we most frequently use and how we can employ virtues, to help us change our inner style and script, to become better role models for the children around us. When a child sees a teacher become frustrated and make a decision that affects everyone in the classroom in a negative way, and they see this behaviour repeated consistently; they adapt this decision making style into their inner decision making script. Children imitate our actions, which can lead to a host of negative consequences. It becomes a pattern of emotionally guided decisions, which creates a behaviour, from which consequences occur creating more emotions. Reflection is never added to the mix. The 9-PAC Integrity Approach Model has a new decision-making cycle: emotion, reflection, gathering of data, objectively observing how the decisions and consequences will affect others behaviour, reflection on the outcome, emotion and enhancing of the virtues used or strengthening other virtues to help change the inner script.

If we use the example above of the teacher who becomes frustrated, a 9-PAC role model would take a deep breath, reflect on why they were angry, talk to the student or students about what their choices are, what the consequences would be, have everyone reflect on how the decisions and consequences will affect others. They then allow the student or themselves, to make a decision. Then there would be reflection time, on the consequences that occurred, because they are not always as we expect them to be and the reflection process, would continue with a look at how the whole process could be done next time, for the betterment of everyone involved.

Can you imagine what the impact on all the people in the world would be, if children and role models worldwide used the 9-PAC Integrity Approach decision-making model? We would see positive change in the world immediately and there would be helpfulness, compassion, friendliness, thoughtfulness, tolerance, and consideration used for every decision that was made. All decisions would come from a 'win–win' perspective, which is very different from the perspective that society now uses. There would be less arguments, more ownership of decisions made and more willingness to admit when decisions did not turn out according to expectation. Consequences could be accepted and changes to character and inner script would happen almost immediately, as each mistake was used as a case study, not for judgement and criticism, but because everyone would feel like they were part of the process and took ownership of the outcomes.

Taking Responsibility

How does an individual take responsibility for their choices and consequences? In the 9-PAC Integrity Approach Model, role models immediately take responsibility for their decisions and consequences, because they took the time to reflect upon the decision-making process, so they owned their choices. They actively look to take responsibility for their choices, so they can reflect upon them to see if the consequences are what they predicted would happen. If the consequences are different, they look to see how and why that happened. They then choose to consciously become more aware of their inner script perceptions and beliefs, through mindfulness during the process, and allow themselves to see where they can evolve their processes, to make better decisions in the future.

Many people baulk at taking responsibility for their actions and will use either blame, excuses or denial to avoid taking responsibility for their decisions. In our society it is easier to blame others for our actions, than to take ownership of the responsibility of our choices. Blaming someone else means a person does not have to face the consequences of their decisions and that they can ignore the outcome of the decision and how it impacted others. When blaming others, individuals do not look internally at how they have contributed to a certain situation, because they don't want to deal with the hurt or suffering, that they cause themselves or others; for a choice that was not well thought out. Blaming others means the blame lies externally with someone else and they believe it has nothing to do with their decision, therefore there is no need to contemplate on any part the individual took in the decision making process.

For instance, a parent may have been playing games on their phone, while their child was on the playground. Because they were not paying attention, their child may have accidentally, or on purpose, pushed another child over resulting in that child getting injured. The other parent may have become angry and verbally abusive towards the game-playing parent and their child. The game-playing parent becomes defensive and verbally abuses the other parent back, even though they have no idea what has really gone on. They are simply reacting emotionally to an event and making a snap decision, and reacting in a responsive way by attacking back. There is a saying that you should never argue with an idiot because people might not know the difference. When two people argue nobody wins. You can't argue with somebody who refuses to argue. Be the one to stop the argument and respond by consulting and if necessary, taking responsibility and apologising. What message does this send to the children? That parents attack other parents, that other children can be mean because a distracted parent was not watching or that the parent who did wrong, was allowed to yell at another parent? Where is the compassion for what actually happened to the hurt child? Where is the responsibility taken, by both parents for one being distracted and both becoming overly emotional and attacking each other?

In this type of role modelling, our pride and ego is more important than anything else. It is easier to get fired up and retaliate and leave the park feeling angry, annoyed and frustrated. But also feel guilt, because deep down, the parent knew they were not paying as much attention to their child, as they should have been. Sometimes it is harder in the moment to stop emotions from taking over and reacting, rather than taking a moment and deciding how to respond. When 9-PAC Integrity Approach role models focus on a virtue each day and take time out for reflection, they consider what the other child and adult are feeling, they decide how to respond based on all the information they can access, they own their choices and they respond with a 'win–win' and teaching mentality. They can diffuse the situation by admitting wrongdoing, apologise, show compassion for the child who got hurt and administer consequences to the child, who hurt the other child. They have their child own up to their choice, by apologising and they explain why the consequences are happening and what they are, so their own child can understand how the choice they made, was not a good choice for everyone involved. After the park experience, they can discuss it with their child and family, see what they and the child could have done things differently next time, to avoid a similar situation. They can choose to listen to different points of view from their family that they may never have considered and decide how both the parent and child can change their inner script, to help them make better decisions in the future.

Communicating, in an assertive nonaggressive, tone and character, is a good way to role model to children the type of behaviour that you would like to see them engage in. You can practice assertive communication honestly, tactfully and with confidence, by letting the child, or children know the consequences of their actions if they conduct themselves in a certain way that is disruptive. For example, I recall a friend of mine who teaches in a high school say that at the beginning of the year she set class rules on what was expected of the students. However, when she walked into a class, the students would ignore her and continue to talk with each other and it was sometimes a battle to get all of them to pay attention to what she wanted to teach. She would get frustrated, raise her voice and this only made the situation worse. One day she decided to change her tactic, she walked into class and once she had prepared herself and was ready to teach, if the talking had not stopped she would stand and patiently look down at her watch, not talking. She calculated that the time it took for her to walk into class and place her tools on the table and write on the blackboard, was enough time for the students to prepare themselves for the lesson, and wind-up their conversations. Her tone and body language told them she expected them to be considerate, thoughtful and respectful toward her, as their teacher. Naturally a few students noticed and asked her what she was doing and she stated that she was keeping an eye on the time, so that she knew how much of her time was being wasted by not teaching them what she needed to, so that she knew how much time she needed to spend with them during their lunch time, so the lesson could be completed. As you can imagine the students stopped talking quickly and encouraged the others to stop talking. The students were told of new consequences to their actions and given the choice on how they wanted to proceed. Giving students choices and consequences that are fully explained to them, teaches them that they are responsible for their actions and that every action has a consequence, which affects not only themselves, but others as well.

In another example, often in primary schools, many students like to 'tell' on each other. A teacher I am acquainted with would take this approach when a student would come up to her with a 'tell'. She would ask if the 'tell' was to get the other student into or out of trouble. This encouraged the student who was 'telling', to think about their purpose and be honest with themselves. Was the information helpful and would it serve both the student and the teacher to know whatever it was, or was the intention just to get the other student in trouble? The class had a set of rules and consequences already on 'telling', so the student was aware of what the consequence was, in trying to get another student into trouble. This reflective question gave the student the opportunity to make a choice, based on what the known consequence was and if they were making a decision, which was a win–win decision. It allowed the student to see how their action could have negative consequences that could that affect themselves and others.

Accepting responsibility opens the door to freedom, as a person no longer feels the need to defend themselves and learns to accept the decision they made and the consequences of those actions. How can a 9-PAC Integrity Approach Role Model help children learn to take responsibility for the decision-making process? It all begins with role modelling the decision-making model to them. When children see you role modelling positive and reflective decision making strategies and they see the outcomes of the win–win mentality. When they see you admitting mistakes and learning from them, children will feel how good this decision making model makes them feel and move towards adopting it into their inner script. The blame game always leads to feeling unworthy, less than and shameful. No one likes to feel this way and when children are consistently presented with a way to make decisions that make them and others feel good, they will move toward adopting this model. It is human nature to want to feel good and to be of service to others.

Consequences are Gifts that Build Character

The best gift you can give another person is an insight into their own behaviour and provide them with an opportunity to contribute to the behaviour they wish to see in their own environment. After sharing my knowledge of virtues with a university lecturer, the different strategies involved in using the virtues, and that it is a tool that is appropriate for all ages, he decided to test it out on his upcoming new class of students. He later informed me that he took along the virtues poster to class and hung it on the blackboard and asked the class what virtues they would like to see in class and how they would like to see that virtue in action. He said everyone came up with ideas and every member of the class put forth a virtue and how they would like to see it displayed. Then together, the class broke it all down and agreed on a limited number of virtues they would like to see in the class. He typed up their agreement and got everyone in the class to sign it. He laminated it and placed it on the board as a reminder, during every lesson. He reported that it was the best class he had taught in regard to student behaviour and that rather than him having to remind the students about talking over each other and technology being inappropriately used, the students themselves reminded each other of the virtues that were not being demonstrated.

The students helped create the rules and the consequences and the students not only enjoyed the subject matter, but attending the lessons with acceptance, an open-minded approach and felt respected and safe in their environment. They self-regulated the behaviour of others who broke the rules, not by yelling or bullying, but by reminding the other person about the virtues, that were picked out as a class. It created an environment that fostered respect. The gift for the teacher was to enjoy providing a stress-free class, which was a consequence to taking the time at the beginning of the year, to empower the students to establish explicit perimeters and consequences to their own actions.

Consequences helped the students in this case learn to create their own respectful environment, where they felt a sense of ownership over it, because they were part of the decision-making process. They helped create their own consequences and rules, through mindful reflection on what virtues they wanted to see in their 'classroom community'. When given a choice most children, students and individuals, will work to see the environment that they helped create, continue to be a place of respect and support. Following along with something you believe in and helped to create, is something that people can stand behind and work towards keeping up and nurturing. When students take ownership over their environments, decisions and lives, they become mindful, reflective and community minded individuals, who work towards the common good. This is because it is something they agreed to and when people agree with something, they work to keep it intact.

Establishing ethical foundations in our children is like building a house, the foundation is the most important and time-consuming part as it is the foundation which supports the entire structure. Just like with a building a person has inner strength that supports every other aspect that happens after the foundation is formed.

Although we don't always know what the outcomes of our actions will be, we can take responsibility and choose to mindfully reflect on what the consequences to our decisions could be and how they will affect not only ourselves, but the people, community and society around us. When we understand our consequences, and see how they affect others around us, we become more mindful of the decision-making process. How much research we have to do to make an informed decision and make reflective choices that we take responsibility for. We have the choice to own our decisions and consequences, instead of playing the blame game and look for the silver lining in each consequence we have to face. When we learn to humbly accept our mistakes, they can be used as vitally important teaching case studies with the children around us. When we use every decision making process as a learning experience we grow spiritually, intellectually and emotionally. There are boundless, gentle moments, during each and every decision-making process, that role models can use to guide a child, to learn how to use the 9-PAC Integrity Approach decision making model.

We all makes mistakes and sometimes it is the mistakes that build our character and, once overcome, provide the insight into recognising the ability within ourselves to help others through similar experiences. For example as mentioned earlier some of the best drug and alcohol counsellors are people who have at some time been addicted to drugs or been alcohol dependent, children who have been abused have grown up to become adults who work tirelessly to catch the people who contribute to this issue, the small mistakes we make each and every day enable us to become stronger in some way. Mistakes happen, they always happen, trust it is for a reason.

When our children and the children that we guide and teach, learn how to make objective, compassionate and mindful decisions, they will become better leaders, teachers and parents in the future. Helping to shape our communities, countries and our world into the place that we truly hope that it will become and that we will feel is a safe and harmonious place to live in. Decisions are key in every life and form literally every moment of our day. When children learn how to make appropriate decisions that take into account others needs and create 'win–win' solutions we all benefit as they integrate this model into their inner script and begin to role model it to others around them. This is where society begins to truly change, when role models and the children in their care are all consistently making decisions in the same positive way, their positive influence spreads. As others feel good around them and are happy with the decision they make on a daily basis. These individuals then begin to also adopt this decision making modality and everyone begins to use the 9-PAC Integrity Approach decision making model and we all begin to once again speak a common language and have common positive scripts. This is how peace in our societies, our communities and our world, can be achieved.

We all are global citizens and our children are naturally compassionate creatures who are not driven by money, ego or power and we often hear about the ideas that form in their creative minds. With the support of their role models come to fruition because they do not see differences in colour, or sexual preference, religion or country of birth or any other discriminatory issues that adults see and participate in. Children want all children to be treated equally and for all children to be supported by their role models. They do not understand why some countries dictate to their citizens their religious or sexual preferences, why some countries have no water readily available, why some people use children as tools for self-gratification. Why some people are cruel and do nasty things to others, why some children in the world do not have access to education or medication, why some people feel that because they were born in a particular place they have the right to services and the privilege to speak their mind and others do not have that same right? We are all responsible for creating, and continuing to allow, all these issues and our children will either become part of the problem or the solution. I believe our children have the solution within them and it is up to us to guide them and support them in the best way that we can so they can offer their gifts to the world which will result in eliminating or reducing these issues as caring, kind, compassionate, accepting and respectful children become the adults of the future.

CHAPTER 5 – SUMMARY

- Decisions should be made with a positive intent

- Providing choices teaches responsibility and is empowering

- Research is key to making objective decisions

- The outcome of your actions is not always known regardless of the amount of research conducted

- Role models and children need to know how their inner script affect their decisions

- Every consequence has a silver lining and is character building

CHAPTER 6

Control

Definition

- To direct the behaviour of (a person or animal): to cause (a person or animal) to do what you want

- To have power over (something)

- To direct the actions or function of (something): to cause (something) to act or function in a certain way

"It always seems

impossible

until it's done."

Nelson Mandela

The Nail in the Fence

The next time you are tempted to say something hurtful to someone just because you're angry, you might want to stop and remember this story: it's a keeper.

There once was a little boy who had a bad temper. His father gave him a bag of nails and told him that every time he lost his temper, he must hammer a nail into the back of the fence.

The first day the boy had driven 37 nails into the fence. Over the next few weeks, as he learned to control his anger, the number of nails hammered daily gradually dwindled down. He discovered it was easier to hold his temper than to drive those nails into the fence.

Finally the day came when the boy didn't lose his temper at all. He told his father about it and the father suggested that the boy now pull out one nail for each day that he was able to hold his temper. The days passed and the young boy was finally able to tell his father that all the nails were gone.

The father took his son by the hand and led him to the fence. He said, "You have done well, my son, but look at the holes in the fence. The fence will never be the same. When you say things in anger, they leave a scar just like this one. You can put a knife in a man and draw it out. It won't matter how many times you say I'm sorry, the wound is still there."

The little boy then understood how powerful his words were.

Unknown

What is control? Can a person control other people? Can they control themselves? Are people in control of their own thoughts and can they control the thoughts and behaviours? How would controlling our thoughts benefit ourselves and society? How do we model self-control to children? In this chapter, I will answer these questions and look at what you can and cannot control in your life and how this impacts yourself and those around you. I will talk about how control can be a detrimental practice, but also how it can also be a positive practice when role models control their thoughts and behaviour. I will talk about how control allows a person to change their inner script, which allows them to become a better 9-PAC Integrity Approach role model.

Control can be closely linked to power, however, the only person you truly have any control over, is yourself. You can have influence over others, but not complete control. People may be able to control other's behaviour, this is true, but they cannot fully control their whole being – their thoughts, ideas, beliefs, attitudes or feelings. There have been many movies made which start with one party trying to control another but throughout they show the strength of the human spirit and how people overcame that control. No one can control a person's beliefs, attitudes and feelings, unless an individual gives them permission to do so and even then, their control is still limited; because the other person can change their inner script, which controls their thoughts, feelings and beliefs, at any time.

Things People Can Control

There are a few things that a person can practice controlling in their life, and the more they practice, the more they will find themselves better able to control their decisions, actions and feeling. To find out how much self-control you have as a role model, you can do this exercise. It can also be done with the children you guide or teach.

Things people can control:

- Their tongue/language/words

- Their thoughts

- Their attitude

- Keeping an open heart and open mind

Tongue:

When we control our words, we are careful about what we say to others and consider if what we are about to say is kind, true and necessary. It is important to say things with kindness and tact, and to be honest. Whatever someone says, will impact on how the other person feels. An individual can increase the other person's happiness by empowering them through language or discourage them, with their words. Controlling our tongue, also means keeping it still and not interrupting others when they are speaking. This is part of engaging in conscious listening, which we talked about in earlier chapters. When role modelling to our children, it is important to use language to help them become more self-aware, acknowledge their strengths of character and assist them in becoming mindful of areas where they could grow and enhance their virtues. This way our children can become confident, independent beings, who live their life, by giving back to the world in a way that fills their heart and soul. Children speak their minds with honesty and no sense of tact. Adults rarely take offence when a child says something, for we often find it amusing, when it comes 'out of the mouth of babes'. However, this same type of brutal honesty can be hurtful to their classmates at school and in their community. It is therefore important to teach our children about honesty, tact and the importance of being kind, when interacting with other children.

Thoughts:

Having control over your mindset is one of the most powerful gifts you can give yourself. Everyone has negative thoughts and they are often about themselves, but these negative thoughts have absolutely no value and yet people waste many hours thinking about them. Negative thoughts lead to negative actions and it causes people to stagnate their growth potential and stalls their ability to contribute to society. When a negative thought comes into a person's mind, about themselves or someone else, the best course of action is to change it into a positive thought. The 9-PAC Integrity Approach Model recommends a person try to think of a minimum of three positive things or positive virtues that they can see within themselves or the other person. By understanding the virtues discussed in Chapter Three, a role model will be able to pick out these virtues in others and also within themselves quite easily. Which allow them to change their negative thoughts into positive thoughts in a short amount of time.

For example, if a child spills milk on the floor just before the parent plans to go to work, the parent can focus on their own virtue of 'flexibility'. When an individual practices flexibility, they become mindful of how they can choose to respond to these types of situations, rather than simply reacting; because they got frustrated or angry with the situation. The parent can then focus on looking at their child's virtues and finding gratitude for the positive virtues and character traits that the child displayed in the situation. Maybe the child was calm when they spilled the milk and maybe they were responsible and told the parent that they had created the spill, immediately. The parent can now focus on these positive character traits and compliment the child on them. This shifts the event from a negative to a positive. When the parent compliments the child on these virtues, it helps to empower the child to continue to keep displaying these virtues, throughout their life.

Taking time for reflection at the end of each day and asking yourself if you looked for three virtues in each person or in yourself, when you felt frustrated, angry or afraid, and did you listen to the answers that you found deep within. This will allow an individual to become more aware of their thought patterns and see if they were mostly positive during the day or tended to lean towards the negative. A person can find balance and moderation in their life if they take control of their thoughts in this way and consciously focus on being positive and find the flow of life. Taking time out for daily reflection or meditation is one of the most effectual habits a person can embody in life. As a person's thoughts become peaceful during these peaceful activities, they are reflected into their daily actions. Consequently, over time, the person's thoughts and actions will become more peaceful and they will be able to pause and reflect on other people's actions and their own thoughts more consistently. Subsequently in stressful moments, they will no longer react, but respond in a peaceful way.

Attitude:

Humans are very complex and there is such a diverse mix of cultural identities in the world, which creates even more complex character traits. Some of the people you will encounter tend to focus on the negative and have very narrow viewpoints and beliefs. They often make decisions based on feelings and emotional triggers, with no reflection on how it impacts the world around them. Other people that we interact with are kind, loving and compassion people. They are people that we can admire and are grateful to have in our lives as role models.

There are times in life when a person wakes up and they just need a little inspiration to crawl out of bed and prepare for their day. They have two options to use on difficult days like this, 1. they can choose to maintain a sense of dread, or 2. reject the negative feelings and thoughts and replace them with something more positive. Having an 'attitude of gratitude' is something that many successful people feel contributes to their sense of wellbeing and joy, and it tends to attract positive events and people into their life. When a person has a positive attitude, it increases their energy level, and they feel more confident and determined to take action and get started on their day.

The 9-PAC Integrity Approach model recommends that when things get tough in life, role models focus on 5–10 things they are grateful for in their life right now. The morning is a very good time to focus on gratitude, in order to start the day off with a positive thought pattern. When a person is grateful for what they have in their life, they often feel that the universe supports them. When they believe this, they continually benefit from, feel appreciative of, and become thankful for, what is happening in their life. When a person controls their attitude towards events and situations they encounter, whether they be positive or negative, they can change their attitude about the event, and it only takes a single thought. I bought a coffee cup that had a saying on it, 'Attitude – pick a good one'. We can always choose how we want to think and feel, and this can help us have a more positive life experience if we choose to direct our thoughts in a positive way.

Open Heart and Open Mind:

Having an open heart, leads to an open mind. Once a person opens their heart, they allow others in, allowing in new ideas, beliefs and perception; which broaden a person's outlook on life and impacts their inner script. Compassion and empathy is a consequence of having an open heart, as it causes an individual to listen to what others are experiencing in their life and accepts them for where they are at on their journey. I recall seeing a video clip that took place in police station, where a knife-wielding man approached a police officer, who rather than pulling his gun on the man, sat down on a desk and started talking to the man and convinced him to hand over his knife. Once the man handed over the knife, the police officer approached the man, not to place handcuffs on him, but to hug him. The consequence of receiving a heartfelt hug resulted in the man expressing his remorse and explaining to the officer the stress that he was under in his life. The police officer then offered to take the man out for a meal before taking the man to hospital for a mental health assessment. No charges were filed and the police officer was praised for his courage and compassion.

By sharing stories such as these with children we guide and discuss what other options and consequences could have taken place, which allows us to educate our children about the different options they can take when dealing with a stressful situation. Children are often able to open their hearts and minds in amazing ways. For example, there have been many stories around the world of children coming up with the idea for hot lunch programs, after noticing that other children did not come to school with a proper lunch or any lunch at all. Other children have created 'pay-it-forward' kindness bracelets to help combat bullying and other children have created life-saving inventions after they lost a sibling in a heartbreaking accident.

Teaching a child about self-awareness also provides the opportunity to have them think about someone that they may not usually think kindly of. The role model can ask the child to search in their heart to see how their heart feels and think about whether it feels open or closed. A role model can guide the child to see that a person can use their wisdom and detachment, when dealing with certain people or situations that they don't like, without closing their heart to them. Wisdom and detachment are virtues that we all need to learn more about, to keep our heart open, as well our minds open to find compassionate and empathetic solutions to society's problems.

Controlling vs Role Modelling

The word control has both negative and positive connotations and it is important to always reflect upon our own behaviour so that an individual recognises within themselves. Whether they are having an internal conflict about the love of power, or the desire to help guide others, in a way that benefits future generations. Control, like everything else in life requires balance and moderation. As a role model guides children, they teach them to become independent, future role models, who make considerate and reflective choices, instead of making choices to control others, to get their own way. An example, we used earlier in the book, a parent let their child choose to have a bath before or after dinner. The parent was 'controlling' the bigger picture, by ensuring that cleanliness was still taking place in the family, but they forgo 'controlling' the smaller choices, of when events are going to happen and allowed the child to make those choices. The parent, was ensuring that the child had a responsible framework to work within, and empowered them to make reflective choices, which taught them responsibility and built their confidence.

Role models can teach children the difference between controlling themselves and controlling others by speaking to them about virtues and discussing everyday situations; where they can choose to practice a specific virtue and then be reflective of its impact, on others and their environment. For example, a teacher could use a book that they have read to their class, where a storybook character tried to control other people, to get their own way. Maybe the character in the book, tried to control other's actions, beliefs or feelings. The teacher can ask the students how they would feel if someone tried to control them, the way the character was trying to control the other characters in the book. They can ask their class to consider why the character was trying to control people, instead of using win–win decision making processes. The class could talk about the immediate consequences to the characters trying to control others and other far reaching consequences of their behaviour, if the character continued to behave in this type of controlling manner. The students could think of a list of virtues that would help the character to change their inner script and how the character could implement them in their life daily. Then the students could each write a new story, on how the character started off trying to control people, but they found a role model who taught them about virtues which helped them become a more empowered individual. Students can continue the story by writing about how that helped the character change their inner script and create new consequences that could happen in the story because of this change.

Children are very resourceful and with the right support, can make a massive difference in their own lives, regardless of age. Children are amazing and can be so creative when they are supported and not given control limits on their skills, talents and mindset. They often see a problem and have a desire to solve it immediately as they don't place limits upon themselves. Children are able to use creative solutions to resolve issues that they encounter. Children 'do', they do not 'try'. They learn as they go along and can benefit greatly, by learning to employ reflection, on their thoughts and decisions. Taking time out for stillness and reflecting on if they practiced a particular virtue and how it made them and others feel, it vital to their learning process. If they can learn through trial and error, reflect on whether they were attempting to control others to get their way and why they felt they had to do this, gives them great practice for adopting this objective mindset, as they go forward in life.

If children can come to believe that 'win–win' solutions are valuable long term for themselves, their communities and society. They will develop strong assertive characters and confidence in their decision-making processes, and no longer use control, as part of their decision-making strategies. This is also true for the role models who guide children – they also need to look deep inside and reflect on their behaviour. If they are attempting to control children, to get what they want, have an easier day or have less stress in their lives. Are they controlling the child, to the point where they limit their potential and creativity? Or are they controlling the acceptable decisions that children can pick from, while being open to other solutions, that come from the children that they may not have considered. Control can help to keep our children safe and secure. If used in an inappropriate way it can be highly detrimental to them especially if role models employ control only to create mini copies of themselves.

An example of a role model who is using control appropriately is a role model who controls the behaviour of a child, so that they do not run out into the street to get a runaway ball. The role model will come up with acceptable choices the child can choose from, such as;

a) going to get a parent, so they can get the ball for them, or

b) stopping and pausing when the ball goes across the road, using a road crossing or crosswalk to go across the road, to be able to get the ball and being very cautious when they cross the road.

The role model is not limiting the child in detrimental ways or forcing them to do things to get their own way, they are creating acceptable choices that the child can choose from. This way the child learns how to deal with a problem in an acceptable and safe manner.

It is important for children to go through their teenage years, with a good understanding of controlling others vs controlling themselves. We all know that as children grow up there is constant peer pressure within some groups regarding smoking, drinking, drug-taking and cultural identities where some 'friends' try to control their friends including how they look, their beliefs and consequently actions concerning sex and other activities. When a child understands how to control their own thoughts, they become aware when others are trying to control them and how to deal with these issues in appropriate ways. They can make choices that take into account everyone involved, but in the end, creates an acceptable consequence.

The more aware, reflective and confident a child, teenager or person feels in themselves, the less likelihood there is of them following or getting involved with someone or a group, that does not have their best interests at heart. Helping them identify when someone is attempting to get them to do something that they are not comfortable with or to simply control them. Children will often make decisions that we as role models may believe is detrimental to them, but it is important that we respect their decisions (as long as it is not drastically hurtful to themselves or others). As we discussed earlier in the book, failure often creates tremendous learning opportunities. With a good mentor helping to guide the children through these challenging years, children will still make mistakes and learn from them but with far less detrimental consequences to themselves, others and our society. We can influence our children through our actions, words and behaviours. We can share our own mistakes with them and what we would have done differently, now that we have better tools and internal scripts, then in our childhood. However, this does not tell them what they have to do, it models to them how we as role models made mistakes and how we learned from them. Using mistakes as a learning tool, will not force a child to behave in a particular way, nor is it an attempt to control their thoughts, feelings and actions. Controlling children strictly for the purpose of making them do what we want is a detrimental form of control that stifles their potential and inhibits them from learning to make confident choices. Helping children understand all the choices available to them and helping them to understand all the data needed to make their decisions, is proper role modelling and is teaching the child about inner control.

It is important for role models to help children learn to not beat themselves up for the mistakes that they make, but to help them see these mistakes as learning opportunities. To help them strengthen or bring a balance of the virtues into their lives, that will help them enhance their character traits and help them to make better decisions for themselves and others in the future. Guiding children is always about helping them become independent, confident adults, who know appropriate behaviours and ways of treating others. Adults who have lots of tools to create 'win–win' situation that have acceptable consequences for others around them and for society. Guiding children is not about creating the child to become a mini-copy of the role model. The 9-PAC Integrity Approach Model, teaches that role models encourage and support children's innate skills, talents and character traits, so that they can become the very best person that they were truly meant to be in this world. Not a copy of someone else, because that will limit their potential and creativity.

How to Control your Thoughts

Our inner script is what a person needs to control, in order to see the positive in themselves and others. As I discussed earlier in the book, positive self-talk, creates a positive internal script. When a person has consistent positive thoughts and self-talk, the world around them changes to become predominantly more positive as well. What we project into the world, is what we get back from it. If we want a utopian society, we need to see and speak positive out into the world and the world will reflect that back to us. It is vital for our society that we start to express the positive in ourselves, to ourselves, as well as the positives that we see in each other, so that we strengthen our resolve regarding who we are and who we want to be. This empowered outlook and character, empowers others around us and our children, to develop their self-awareness and self-confidence; by learning that they can also control their future by constructing an optimistic inner script. This assists them to become whatever they choose to become in this world and helps them to make a favourable impact on the world, with their skills, talents and abilities.

For example, a primary school teacher could ask their class to think about how it would feel to go to a new school and not know anybody.

They could ask the students to visualise how would they like to be treated and how their inner self-talk would be affected, if students in this new school were mean to them. This allows the students to reflect on how they would like others to treat them, helping them learn how to treat other children around them, in a compassionate way. The class could think about how a negative inner script, would affect their behaviour when interacting with students in the new school and how a positive inner script would also affect their behaviour. The teacher could discuss the virtues of friendliness, helpfulness, kindness, courage and unity and ask the students to describe when they have experienced these virtues themselves or had these virtues modelled to them, by others. The students could come up with examples of how these virtues could be implemented into in their daily lives and how it would make them feel if they practiced these virtues. They could talk about how they would feel if others practiced these virtues when they interacted with them. The teacher could finish the exercise by explaining how when we choose to embody these virtues, we are choosing to control our thoughts and behaviours, to become a more positive influence in our families, communities and schools.

Helping children to discovering their inner strength and whether their inner script is predominately positive or negative and if they try to control others to get their way or help to empower others is a wonderful way to have them become more self-aware. When a person's inner script is more positive than negative, they gradually recognise and acknowledge themselves on a daily basis. They will find that they feel good about themselves and who they are and who they want to be. When who they are and who they want to be is aligned they feel good about themselves which strengthens their inner script. This allows them to be in a better position to overcome life's challenges much more quickly and with more ease, than if they did not have a strong inner script or positive self-worth. It is the inner script that each person can control, through regular practice, and the inner script that gives individuals immense control in their life. This is because when a person controls their inner script and what virtues they choose to embody, it affects their thoughts, beliefs, opinions, emotions and behaviours.

Always see from your heart also as sometimes people seem to attempt to control you because they want you to do something that they enjoyed or that brought them joy. Rather than feeling irritated by someone who appears pushy consider what their intention is and if you believe it to be pure then thank them for their concern and stick to what feels right for you at that moment in time. It takes strong inner strength to handle situations when friends, acquaintances or colleagues are continually pushing for you to do something that does not feel right for you at that moment. Be true to yourself and follow your path so that your desire leads to your destiny.

Older children can learn to control their inner script by learning how they can contribute to their family, class/school and society, by becoming responsible for themselves. This could include unpacking their lunchboxes and drink containers when they get home each evening, placing their school notes in a specific spot inside their school bags and remembering do their homework, without needing to be reminded. They can learn to help plan their lunch menus for the week and even help to make their own lunches, with guidance from their parents. This teaches them to be in control of where their things are when they need them, rather than feeling anxious and stressed out, which may transfer onto the family also because they could not find their things. By having a conversation with children and helping them to understand the benefits of putting things away and taking on some responsibility for certain aspects of their life, on a frequent basis, this gradually helps them learn to become a responsible adult, who practices orderliness, consideration and thoughtfulness and is able to function on their own; without needing someone to do everything for them. It also helps them to learn to take responsibility for their own successes and mistakes. Focussing on one characteristic or one virtue each day has a positive impact on a child's beliefs about themselves and enables them to know who they are and who they want to be as they grow up. It helps them to continually move in the direction they want to in life and strengthens their inner script. A positive, compassionate and responsible inner script is powerful beyond words and the 9-PAC Integrity Approach Model skills and strategies will benefit them throughout their life's journey.

There are four ways we can control our inner script, our:

- Thoughts
- Action
- Beliefs
- Journey

Thoughts:

Your thoughts come before your actions and are often created by the emotions you feel. Each thought has a degree of substance and level of energy to it that determines how strongly you feel about each thought. Actions follow thoughts, and if the thought has a strong energy to it and a strong emotion behind it, it is more likely that the thought will become an action. A way to help children become more reflective, is to have them focus on one virtue each morning and taking the time to talk about that the virtue means to them and how they would like to model it in their life, for that day. At dinner, they could talk about how modelling the virtue went during the day, how it made them feel to practice that virtue and if they noticed other children or adults around them, modelling that virtue. The child could then talk about how they could embody that virtue in their life going forward. This helps them start to live, interact with others and react from a mindful inner script and not interact with people from a reaction based approach.

Actions:

If we teach children about character traits, virtues and how being mindful of our personal strengths and weaknesses enables us to recognise opportunities to improve and enhance these traits, it helps a child to live life to their fullest potential. It is said that, "In just having awareness, you are halfway there," because it helped you recognise the times in life when you behave in ways that hindered you, but also in ways that helped you. What action is about is having awareness of our inner script, our virtues and traits and putting them to use, when we interact with those around us, in both happy and stressful situations. People see our actions first and then hear our words. How often do children model our behaviour, when we had wished they had modelled our words instead? There is a saying that, "Actions speak louder than words." Imagine a business executive wanted to cultivate respect in his daughter's inner script but he consistently paid the women in his company less, do you think his daughter would feel that the words and actions of her father match and that he values females as much as males, especially when doing exactly the same job? The goal as a 9-PAC Integrity Approach role model, is to have our thoughts, actions and words all match, so that we are consistent when we role model to our children. This is all determined by our inner script and how self-confident and mindful we are, of acting and speaking with the virtues we have chosen to embody in our life.

Beliefs:

There are times when even though you want to act in a particular direction and your thoughts are in line with your goals, your beliefs may not be as solid and as strong as you would like them to be, because you have conflicting beliefs in your inner script. When this happens, you may feel judgemental about yourself and tend to engage in negative self-talk. For example, you may want to start a fitness routine, but may lie in bed and not go for the walk or the run that you planned to do. This could be because of something in the back of your mind that desperately wants you to stay snug and warm in bed. What causes these conflicting beliefs? When your beliefs and actions do not act as one entity it results in procrastination, which is always a good indicator time is needed for reflection and your inner script requires strengthening.

Where do most of your beliefs come from? As stated in previous chapters, they come from watching role models, parents and caregivers as children and embodying their beliefs, ideas and actions into our inner script. Beliefs also come from our cultural identity groups. As a 9-PAC role model, we need to investigate where these beliefs come from and consider whether we took on other people's beliefs, without questioning them. Are we running an inner script that we just copied from our role models and did not consciously choose?

For example, I recall being in a group setting where a young man was in his fourth year of university was studying medicine, so that he could become a doctor. He wasn't too far from finishing his degree and he felt that he had to share something with his parents that he thought would break their heart. He stated that he did not want to become a doctor. He said he never wanted to be a doctor, but assumed that in order to please his parents and his community cultural identity, he should go to school to become a doctor. The father of the young man was also in the room and also shared with the group that he and his wife only supported and encouraged their son to become a doctor because they thought that was what he wanted to do. They just wanted him to be happy and they wanted to be 100% supportive of whatever he chose to do. The young man could have lived his life, unhappily, as a doctor, because of assumptions he made about his parents. There are many times in life when people do things because of something they assumed to be true. These assumptions can cause hurt and consequences that can be detrimental for the person and for the people around them.

Fortunately, this man shared his feelings with his family and changed careers. But he could have wasted 20 years of his life, doing a job that he did not find satisfying and this could have led to the consequences of him resenting his parents and possibly destroying a future marriage; out of unhappiness and pain within his inner script and in his heart. It is important to be honest with ourselves and clarify if what we believe is true for us, or true for others. The serenity prayer comes in handy to remember as he had the wisdom and courage to make changes in his life. When we can become clear if our beliefs are an assumption or a belief we consciously chose to adopt, we can then choose to either act on these beliefs or change them. When we change our beliefs, we change our inner script and consequently our thoughts and actions.

Journey:

A very big choice in life is that a person can choose to be guided by their hopes and dreams, rather than by their fears and doubts. A child can wonder, 'How far can I go?' and feel excited and inspired, rather than allowing themselves to be limited by assumptions and beliefs that are not theirs or negative self-talk. As the poem at the beginning of Chapter Four implies, you just need the take the next step that leads you in the direction that you want to take. In an analogy, picture a road filled with fog. The fog is so thick, the person can hardly see in front of them. They can barely see the next section of road and every time the car moves forward a little more, the next section comes into view. Life is like that, there are seasons in our lives when we have trouble seeing clearly and when we feel like stopping, because we are too scared to move forward, because we cannot clearly see the road ahead. However, when we have a positive inner script, are aware and reflective of our thoughts, beliefs and actions, and when we are clear on our intention, we can move forward through life swiftly. Because we know exactly where we want to go and ask others for help to get there. We make positive decisions that create 'win–win' situations and the road becomes clearer, with each compassionate and mindful interaction we have with others and also with our inner self and voice. This is what true control of self looks like. A person knows who they are, what their strengths and their weaknesses are, and how they want to enhance these strengths by focusing on specific virtues to display in their life. Their thoughts, beliefs and actions align and the person role models consistent, positive and objective character traits and actions.

Most people and children want to live in a peaceful world and interact with others in positive ways that make everyone feel good. We can all do this, by helping children learn to take control of their inner script, language and actions. We can speak to them about their emotions and how to recognise when they are tired or need some time alone, so they do not get to a cranky and short tempered phase that affects others with hurtful words and actions. 9-PAC Integrity Approach role models can teach a child to be in control, by recognising the emotions that they experience, become reflective of what they feel, mindful of how they make choices and reflect on the consequence of those choices. This will allow them to have a better understanding of what the possible outcomes to their actions might be.

The more responsibility a child takes in regard to their self-talk and inner script, the more they feel they are in control of their own life. It is ironic that taking no responsibility for your life or inner script would seem like the easy way out. While taking responsibility for your own thoughts, beliefs and actions, is actually the easier road in life. Practicing compassion, tolerance and mindfulness, will get you further in life and help you to succeed in your dreams and goals. Like grandma always used to say, "You get more bees with honey than you do with vinegar."

Teaching children about taking control of their characteristics, teaches them to respect other people's opinions, even when they differ from their own and to investigate issues for themselves, in order to make up their own mind about what beliefs they want integrate into their inner script. Children learn to be flexible, as the more they learn, grow and make mistakes, the more they clarify who they are and who they want to become.

In the next chapter, we will discover how control and consciousness work together or conversely to prevent a person or child from moving forward in their life. We will look at how awareness and awakening make up our consciousness and how this helps us step into our personal power.

CHAPTER 6 – SUMMARY

- The only person you have any control over is yourself, you only have influence over others

- Procrastination is an indicator that your beliefs and actions are in conflict with each other

- Constantly strengthen your inner script by focussing on a daily virtue

- You control your tongue, thoughts, attitude, actions, open heart and open mind

- Beliefs can be taken from other role models in childhood but they can be changed and adapted

- Controlling yourself is a lifelong challenge and journey

Control, Consciousness, Community

Consciously controlling ourselves prospers
our community

CHAPTER 7

Culture

Definition

- The beliefs, customs, arts, etc., of a particular society, group, place or time

- A particular society that has its own beliefs, ways of life, art, etc.

- A way of thinking, behaving, or working that exists in a place or organisation (such as a business)

"Education is the most powerful weapon which you can use to change the world."

Nelson Mandela

The Old Mule

Once upon a time a farmer owned an old mule who tripped and fell into the farmer's well. The farmer heard the mule braying and was unable to figure out how to bring up the old animal. It grieved him that he could not pull the animal out. He'd been a good worker around the farm. Although the farmer sympathised with the mule, he called his neighbours together and told them what had happened. He had them help haul dirt to bury the old mule in the well and quietly put him out of his misery.

At first, the old mule was puzzled, but as the farmer and his neighbours continued shovelling and the dirt hit his back, he had a thought: he ought to shake off the dirt and step up. And he did just that.

"Shake it off and step up… shake it off and step up… shake it off and step up." Even though he took painful blows of dirt and fought panic, he just kept right on shaking it off and stepping up!

It wasn't long before the old mule stepped up and over the lip of that well. What could have buried him actually blessed him all because of the manner in which he handled his adversity.

Author Unknown

Cultural identity is a feeling of belonging to a group. It is the values, beliefs, thoughts, perceptions and behaviours that are shared by a group of people and are characteristic of this group. This 'cultural identity' ensures the group's survival and helps people feel like they belong and are accepted into this group. It is a person's frame of reference, creating a large part of their inner script and affects their characteristics and personality. It can help a person relate to the world around them and help them learn how to behave appropriately, so they fit into their family unit, community and society with greater ease. It can help an individual have a stable point of reference to refer to, when they are uncertain of what to think, how to make decisions and or what actions to take. Cultural identity can be related to nationality, ethnicity, religion, social class, generation, locality or any kind of group that has its own way of thinking and behaving.

In this chapter I will discuss how cultural identity creates a child's identity at an individual, communal and societal level. Looking at how cultural values can empower or disempower children and how a community's cultural identity can affect a child's inner script and decision-making abilities. I will also discuss how cultural identity can affect role model's behaviours and thoughts, and how the 9-PAC Integrity Approach Model can bridge the gap between differing cultural identities.

Cultural identity is created through the language, social structures, gender orientation and cultural patterns that a child learns from their parents or caregivers. It includes the foods people eat, the verbal and non-verbal expressions people in the group use, their sense of humour and their attitude towards learning. It consists of how these people treat other people, how they view others who are different to themselves, how they treat the elderly and people of different genders and how they interact with and care for their environment.

Children often take on the cultural identity of their parental role models, so that they can fit into their family unit more easily, have their needs met and find the approval they seek. Cultural identity helps children to learn to create their inner script, through watching their parents and caregivers, role model characteristics, virtues, beliefs, behaviours and by watching them make decisions and accept consequences. Cultural identity can be both positive and negative on the development of a child's inner script. They may not be able to eat certain foods, work in certain jobs and they might not be able to talk to different genders or classes of people. Certain roles may be expected of them and they may have limits placed on what they are allowed to strive for in their lives. They may even have limits on what they can look like and how they should behave, if they are a certain gender. This greatly affects a child's inner script because they learn their characteristics, personality traits and virtues from their role models and if their role models only see the world from a specific cultural identity, then the child forms a very limited inner script and way of seeing the world.

For example, a child may have grown up with a low socioeconomic cultural identity. The beliefs prevalent in this community's identity might include – the idea that people cannot get ahead in life, that they must work hard to get very little back, that people in authority cannot be trusted and that they should think and behave in aggressive ways. A child who lives in this cultural identity, may believe that they cannot excel at certain areas in life, such as get a high paying-high education job. They may also believe that they must act out against authority figures in order to survive and that shame and blame are correct behaviours. This same child may then move to a new town, with a different socioeconomic cultural identity and would experience a cultural identity shock, because the people around them do not behave, think or have the same opinions as they do. This causes them to no longer have a frame of reference to work from and they must adapt into a new environment in order to fit in. The other children in this community believe they can become anything they want to become, they believe that people in authority are good role models to follow and they have a positive outlook on life. If the child stayed in the new cultural area for an extended period of time, their inner script would change and they would begin to shift their ideas, thoughts, opinions and values and have a completely new way of looking at the world. This would also increase their self-confidence and self-esteem.

In another example, a particular national culture, may not believe it is appropriate for a female to work, interact with individuals of the male gender and they may only be allowed to wear certain clothing. A child from another national culture may have no limits put upon them and may be free to interact with whomever they wish, take whatever job they wish, and wear whatever they wish. Both children may have the same character traits of compassion, kindness, loyalty and patience, but their cultural identity will shape the way these virtues are viewed and displayed. It will shape how they make choices and what their understanding of consequences will be. Cultural identity shapes our language, communication style, our understanding and practicing of virtues, how we make decisions, how we understand consequences and how we role model.

Our early caregiver role models can shape our inner script in very strong ways, which affects our thoughts, behaviours and decisions. An example of this is the *Australian Story*, an Australian television program that has many examples of people overcoming adversity in their lives and changing their cultural identity and inner script. Vincent Shin, for example, grew up in an environment where his father was physically violent towards his mother, and as he grew up, he also became the target of his father's anger. As a child, he did not understand why his mother did not leave his father, as he did not understand the cultural identity beliefs surrounding domestic violence in the area in which he grew up. Domestic violence, which is not only physical, but psychological social and verbal abuse, was and still is, to some degree, a taboo subject within Australian society with many people still not wanting to talk about it or admit when abuse happens.

Consequently, Victor embodied these violent character traits that he saw being role modelled, because no one show him other ways to behave or modelled that this type of behaviour was not acceptable. He became a difficult student who showed aggression and was often explosive and would raise his voice in anger. Victor stated 'that too much was going on in his head and he was just striving to survive on a day to day basis', school work was the last thing on his mind. Naturally his group of friends became like-minded people who had similar issues and role models in their lives and therefore, he spiralled downwards and received very low grades in school. One day Victor decided enough was enough, and made the decision to further his adult education and despite his low grades years before, he went on to become Australia's first school lawyer. He now teaches children about criminal law, including sexting, while also supporting them emotionally and being a role model for positive behaviour and mindset changes.

Everybody makes choices in their life and although Victor was influenced by the domestic violence within his family at an early age and it affected his inner script in detrimental ways, his innate inner personality traits and virtues allowed him to overcome these issues and to take action to improve his situation. Victor stated 'that opening up about his past was the hardest thing he had to do, but it was also the best thing he could have done for himself'. Despite the role modelled weakness that created his inner script, he enhanced his innate virtues, to become his strength!

As a 9-PAC Integrity Approach role model we can help children change their inner scripts, no matter what their individual cultural identity is, because the virtues used in the 9-PAC Model transcends all cultures. Kindness, compassion, tolerance, reflection, awareness, mindfulness, love, respect and integrity, are virtues that all cultural identities worldwide can agree are positive character traits for children to have. When 9-PAC role models work with and guide children, they see what the child's cultural identity is and how it might have shaped their inner script, but they go beyond this identity to see the child's innate skills, virtues and talents and help them to enhance them, making them shine. Most cultural identities in the world would view a child who learns to make aware and mindful decisions as a positive character trait. Of course, there may be a few exceptions, but overall, good decision-making abilities are held in high regard in most cultural identity groups.

The 9-PAC Model becomes the bridge that creates a common ground, a common language and a common set of ways to role model. Enabling all parents, teachers and caregivers, to help children no matter what their background or cultural identity is: grow and shine.

Cultural Identity at a Community Level

Cultural identity at a community level is made up of many everyday things that you may not have given much thought to. You may speak one specific language, such as English, Italian, Turkish or Malayalam, or you may understand and speak more than one language, depending on whether you have multicultural parents or role models in your life. You may read in English which is read from left to right or you might read in Arabic, which is read from right to left. Each community, school and family unit, has their own cultural identity and each has different beliefs, perceptions and appropriate forms of behaviour. Every nation is made up of vast numbers of different types of community cultural identities that come from different ethnicities, nationalities and religions. Cultural identity on a community level can help children feel accepted, loved, supported and respected for who they are and what they have to offer within their community. However, community cultural identity can also separate them, define them and limit them.

A child who is part of the Asian community living in Australia, may have a cultural identity belief that school and learning is of the utmost importance. They not only go to regular school, they go to an after-school program as well to learn to write Mandarin and learn more about math, science and economics. This separates them from their Australian cultural identity friends who leave school and go to the beach or go to after school activities and don't understand why their Asian community friends cannot come with them. Neither cultural identity is right or wrong, it is simply different.

The 9-PAC Integrity Approach Model can help children learn to bridge the gap between their cultural identity differences, by helping them learn to view each other's differences as strengths of character and not as things that separate each other. Role model parents and teachers can help children see each other's strengths. How another child's knowledge and ways of viewing the world can help them in their lives and how to find wonder in learning about another's cultural identity instead of seeing it as something to be afraid of. The parent or teacher could discuss how the Asian community student's skills with math could help their classmates to excel, with tips and ideas they learned at their other school. The teacher could have the Australian community children, help the other children learn more about different sports and water activities that are abundant in their location and help them learn how to participate in them and learn the rules. Both sets of students get to become role models for their classmates and differences become strengths.

Cultural identity can create a very challenging task for teachers or childcare educators. An individual should ask themselves, what cultural identity do I role model to the children I guide? Is it my own cultural identity, the school's identity or the community's identity being modelled? In actuality, it is a mix of all of them, because we think and act from our inner script, which is formed from all of these cultural identities that we engage in or are a part of. The challenges arise when a child or several children, have very different cultural identities. Each with their own unique style of communicating, different values and traits, as well as different ideas, beliefs and behaviours. Are their inner scripts and cultural identities better or worse than our own? Neither, as a 9-PAC Integrity Approach role model, individuals need to be able to be objective, tolerant and compassionate of all inner scripts and cultural identities of the children they interact with. When role models are able to see the child for who they really are, their innate traits and skills and their innate characteristics and virtues, they are able to help them to enhance these traits or shift them, to help them to become more well-rounded individuals.

As a 9-PAC Integrity Approach role model, we help children to create a kind, caring, compassionate and purposeful cultural identity, by being aware of our own thoughts and behaviours and by taking the time to reflect on how we speak to and treat people and children throughout the course of our day. When we become aware of what our own inner script is and how we react to others who have unfamiliar cultural identities from our own, we are able to see how we can become more tolerant of the differences around us. We can role model these tolerances and mindful choices to the children around us, so they can also learn to be more tolerant of diverse cultural identities. As role models, we teach our future citizens about morals and values that go beyond cultural identity, to a much larger social identity of compassion and tolerance for all things.

The family unit, our community and the cultural identity we associate with, is created from small everyday choices and consequences. As role models, we need to be aware of how our distinct cultural identities, be it family, work, community or ethnic identity, contradict themselves and create confusion in the minds of our children, or the children we guide. A business owner may have a daughter and they want her to feel valued and respected, but at work, they pay their female employees a lower rate because they are using a cultural identity belief that it is okay to pay a woman less for her work. They are using a business cultural identity belief to keep their expenditures at a minimum, while telling their daughter that she should receive equal treatment. This sends a mixed message and our behaviour is always seen as the stronger type of role modelling and integrated faster than what message we communicate to our children.

Parents, teachers, childcare educators and all adult role models, are the only resources that our children have, in ensuring the advancement of our civilisation, and each and every one of us makes an impact. Every community culture has its pluses and minuses. Children learn from observing what each community culture does best and can adapt it into their inner script, which will create our global culture. The broader our thinking, the broader our understanding of each cultural identity and the more respectful we are to everyone around us. Some ways of life may not seem acceptable to others, but the first step in creating a better world is to get to know more about each other's lives and cultures and the reasons people do things; instead of criticising and judging each other's differences. Other people have been taught what is acceptable and valued in their own culture and it may be totally different, to what we were taught was acceptable. But when we take the time to try to mindfully and objectively learn about other's cultural identities, we can bridge the gap and find understanding and tolerance.

We, as 9-PAC role models, can help children learn to bridge this gap, by helping them learn to be reflective and open-minded, when viewing other's differences and this starts with how we role model our reactions to others who are different to ourselves, and the children we guide. Do we respect other cultures, do we open our minds and try to learn about them or do we judge what we don't understand, from our limited perspective? Do we reach out to others and ask about their culture and identity or do we avoid talking to them, or worse yet, do we ridicule them? Little by little we can teach children to learn about each other and most importantly, learn to think independently.

Teachers and parents can do this by teaching children about different cultures around the world and how and why they dress as they do, eat the foods they do, worship in certain ways and treat others with either respect or disrespect. When children begin to learn what creates other people's inner scripts, they can begin to have compassion and understanding for people different from themselves and treat other's differences with interest and reflection, not hostility and fear. Teachers and parents can help children to learn about a specific culture through a case study type of format. They can study all aspects of the culture, how it was formed, why people think and behave the way they do, how it has changed over time and what virtues, character traits and beliefs, do people from this culture have? They can look at how people from this culture made decisions, how their cultural identity is different than theirs and look at the strengths that this cultural identity has. This will help the child learn about a culture that is different to theirs and encourage them to become more self-aware. This will create a worldwide cultural awareness and appreciation for things that are different.

Children are naturally curious of things that are different to their own culture and when we teach them in a case study format, they learn about a culture holistically and can begin to see how inner scripts are formed in that cultural identity and how people will think different then they do. Once they understand how people's inner scripts or stories are created they also understand how theirs were formed and can detach their 'story' from themselves and realise that their past does not define their future and that they can make a choice to change things that they wish to change about their lives. The children are then able to ask about other's ideas and beliefs and seek advice from others, to create solutions that work for everyone. The more children broaden their awareness, the more knowledge they gain and the more confidence they feel within themselves. They also learn to reflect gratefully on the things that they have in their lives that come from the community and cultural identity that they belong to.

Cultural Identity at a Society Level

The positive behaviour we as a society want to see in our communities and nations, is largely the responsibility of adult role models. When we help to nurture children's inner scripts, we help to create a cultural identity, which through their thoughts, actions and decisions, creates the world we all wish to live in. Our tone as role models, our objective demeanour, as well as our mindful and reflective approach to interacting with children, helps to create a societal cultural identity that will benefit all individuals worldwide; regardless of their specific cultural identity.

By choosing to be a 9-PAC role model, you mindfully choose to grow in awareness each day. You observe other people's problems around you and their concerns, and often discover that their problems may be similar to your own issues and concerns. You begin to realise that your differences are not quite so different after all, and that you can be of service to the other person. This increases your self-confidence and fosters compassion for other people in the world. It begins to create a social cultural identity of a 'we' mindset, instead of a 'me' mindset.

Children may or not may be proud of their cultural heritage or identity, depending on what their peer-pressure group or school cultural identity dictates is appropriate. A child from a distinct cultural identity group, growing up in an English-speaking country, may not want to speak the mother language of their own country if their friends do not speak their mother language. Children may feel ashamed of the kinds of foods that are packed in their lunchboxes, because it is different from their friend's food. This can impact a child's inner script in detrimental ways and cause them to feel separated from the school cultural identity that they are a part of.

Children long to be the same and to fit in and be included, rather than excluded. Is this because children start to pick on each other, once they start to see differences between them and they have been taught to think that this is a negative thing rather than a positive thing. Children often hear adult role models speak about other adults, usually in a backbiting manner, and it often involves what is different about another person. This impression of differences being negative things is passed onto the children and they begin to view other cultural identities, with judgement and resentment, rather than wonder and interest. If children did not hear adults talking negatively about other adults and their cultural identities, would they react differently to other children, when they start to discover the differences between them? Would society and its cultural identity change, if we all were more compassionate and tolerant toward one another?

When you ask two children who are friends what is difference between them, they are likely to come up with answers that are very different to what an adult would have observed. Instead of seeing physical differences, they may talk about what they are and are not allowed to do, what they eat that is different from their friends, because of their personal likes or dislikes rather than the culture of the food, and how their friend says certain words differently. Children see things from an internal perspective of 'me' and how I fit into my cultural identity group. Difference can create pride in children, but also low self-worth.

Children instinctively know that if they fit in, they will not get singled out and they will not get bullied. Adults know this as well in society and this forms the societal cultural identity in most cities, territories and nations. When a person stands out, they are often ridiculed to get them to start behaving in appropriate ways that the societal cultural identity believes is appropriate. For example, in a strict Muslim country, wearing a tie-dye tank top, cut off jean shorts and no shoes, would be considered inappropriate. But what makes things appropriate in a society? Doesn't each culture, each community and each family group, see the societal cultural identity in very different ways?

As discussed, cultural identity at any level, is made up of a group of individuals, who have common beliefs, thoughts, perceptions, opinions and behaviours that they all agree upon, often unconsciously, and act in ways that supports these traits; in order to keep the 'Identity' functioning. However, this seeming weakness in our society can become a positive. When people change their ideas, beliefs and actions, the societal cultural identity also changes. This is what the 9-PAC Integrity Approach Model hopes will happen as more role models worldwide begin to change their own cultural identity, inner scripts and begin to speak with a new 9-PAC common language. Empowering the children that they parent or guide; to become mindful, reflective and compassionate towards others and their differences.

When families are created because two people come together as one, then their differences, which were once attractive to each other, can become cause for dissension later on. For example, one difference may be religious beliefs, but when the two individuals focus on virtues and character traits, rather than beliefs, then the family wins, as their child learns about different viewpoints and respect for both ways is shown by all family members. By being respectful of each other's beliefs and by integrating with people of all cultures and belief systems, as long as they are for the betterment of the world, we all stand united and can live peacefully as one.

The 9-PAC Integrity Model hopes that role models will learn to look beyond cultural identity and see the character trait strengths in any child or individual and focus on those strengths. Teach positive decision-making skills and speak words of encouragement and empowerment so that children can learn to increase their confidence and excel in their lives. When we begin to speak in a 9-PAC common empowering language and role model positive virtues and traits, children regardless of their cultural identities, respond in similar ways. They begin to work together, to learn from each other, work toward creating win–win solutions and use their compassion and creativity to make decisions that have appropriate consequences for all people; no matter what their cultural identity is. They begin to change the fabric of the societal cultural identity, because they work together, using each other's strengths to create things, that their judgements and 'me' mindset, could not. Together we are stronger, when we use our combined character strengths, skills and abilities, we function much better as a society and create positive, lasting change in the world.

For example, look at groups of children from nations all over the world that get together for science fairs or computer challenges. Children from many diverse backgrounds work together in harmony, using each other's strengths to create amazing things, because they instinctively know that everyone can bring something to the table, that can help the project or serve the world. Each individual is a puzzle piece that can make up our utopian society and each piece is vital to the whole. If we work together to create harmony, the puzzle comes together with ease and it is a joyful process. The 9-PAC Integrity Approach model aims to teach all role models how to help children learn to work together to help create a better world for all of us and to create a better world for future generations. Each of us can be part of the solution because of our innate character traits and strengths, but we need to also accept that others have complementary skills and talents that we need to help ourselves shine to our fullest potential.

When everyone, no matter what their family, community or cultural identity happens to be, makes a conscious choice to think positively of others, to work in cooperation with others and to actively want to learn about other inner scripts and cultural differences, we create an amazing pool of talent, ideas and solutions that individual people could not come up with on their own. Different perspectives create different solutions and when a win–win mentality is kept as the intention, society changes in incredible ways and people naturally seek to work together and continue to keep the harmonious direction going. The 9-PAC Integrity Approach Model can help role models bridge the gap between cultural identity differences and see them as potential strengths of character and opportunities to grow and learn from each other. When many people in our society role model the 9-PAC Integrity Approach Model to children, our future begins to change in exciting and beautiful ways that will help to ensure a positive and peaceful future for humanity.

CHAPTER 7 – SUMMARY

- Children long to fit into the cultural identities around them, to feel safe, secure and to fit in, in order to get their needs met

- Cultural identity is shared beliefs, thoughts, perceptions and actions held by a group of people and contributes to a child's inner script, personality and character

- No one's cultural identity is better than another's. We all have differences that can be seen as strengths of character and can be used to help each other when we work together.

- Individual cultural identity is initially created in children, through absorbing their parents or caregivers cultural identity

- People can change their cultural identity by leaving the cultural identity group they are part of or changing their internal script

- Individual and community cultural identity make up our societal cultural identity such as schools, interest groups, religion and ethnicity

CHAPTER 8

Consciousness

Definition

- The condition of being conscious: the normal state of being awake and able to understand what is happening around you

- A person's mind and thoughts

- Knowledge that is shared by a group of people

"Very little is needed to
make a happy life,
it is all within yourself
in your way of thinking."

Marcus Aurelius

Your hearts know in silence the secrets of the days and the nights.

But your ears thirst for the sound of your heart's knowledge.

You would know in words that which you have always known in thought.

You would touch with your fingers the naked body of your dreams.

And it is well you should.

The hidden well-spring of your soul must needs rise and run murmuring to the sea;

And the treasure of your infinite depths would be revealed to your eyes.

But let there be no scales to weigh your unknown treasure;

And seek not the depths of your knowledge with staff or sounding line.

For self is a sea boundless and measureless.

Say not, "I have found the truth," but rather "I have found a truth."

Say not, "I have found the path of my soul." Say rather, "I have met the soul walking upon my path."

For the soul walks upon all paths.

The soul walks not upon a line, neither does it grow like a reed.

The soul unfolds itself like a lotus of countless petals.

Kahlil Gibran

Consciousness is complex, it includes being aware of many things such as our thoughts, beliefs, intentions, actions, environment, strengths, weaknesses, feelings and emotions, and how they impact on our lives. Consciousness is made up of how aware and awake an individual is, to why they think and act the way they do. Awareness is knowing what makes up our inner script and character, how we communicate, make choices, face consequences and fit into our cultural identity. Awakening is the journey of discovery about ourselves, our constant evolution and our ongoing development, physically, spiritually, emotionally and intellectually.

Our inner script is learned from our early childhood role models and from experiences with other people and situations we face in our life. It is created from our self-talk, our positive or negative thoughts and the words of others we allow into our hearts. Our inner script is both subconscious and conscious. Most people's inner script is subconscious, they do not take the time to reflect on their character traits, abilities, beliefs, perceptions and patterns. Once we begin to practice reflection on a daily basis, by practicing a virtue a day, it allows us to dive deep into our inner script and see what characteristics and personality traits we want to keep and which ones we want to shift and evolve.

Communication is the foundation of our conscious and subconscious beliefs. In other words what we hear spoken to us and what we speak to ourselves forms the beliefs that we hold, which drive our actions. Positive communication creates self-confident children who are assertive, compassionate, objective and use positive decision-making processes. They admit when they make mistakes and they accept the consequences of their well thought out decisions and use these mistakes as learning opportunities. Negative communication instils fear, low self-worth, low self-esteem and a reluctance to making decisions of any kind in children. Some people very rarely admit to making mistakes and refuse to accept any of the consequences or decisions they made or refused to make, so another individual had to choose for them.

Educating our children to be continuously self-aware of their thoughts and actions and practice living in the present moment, teaches them to step into the power of being conscious of everything they do. This allows them to see how their words and actions affect the people and situations around them. They can see how they are making a difference in the world and how they are being of service to their communities and society.

The minute you learn something you cannot unlearn it. There is an awakening that happens inside of you, that may cause you to become curious to explore the topic which created this awakening. For me it was The Virtues Project™. Our conscious and subconscious is impacted by the power of words that we hear. They deeply impact children and once I understood how important it was to communicate in a way that was supportive, encouraging, empowering and respectful, I began to understand the power that communication had over inner scripts. I learned that by meeting children and other individuals, where they were at in their life, I began to understand how positive words empower and create confidence and how negative words can damage a person, their self-talk and their personality. The consequences those negative words have on a child, and everything else I learned throughout my life, caused me to have a driving need to help role models to learn to speak a common empowering language that would help children become kind, caring and compassionate members of society, and that this language needed to be spoken consistently in all corners of the world.

What we will explore in this chapter, is how an awareness of virtues impacts an individual's consciousness and contributes to their awareness of their behaviour. The choices a person makes has consequences, which leads to the creation of the cultural identity group in which the person participates. Consciousness exists at an individual, family, community and societal level, but it all begins with the individual. Individuals are the essential components that make up our societal whole when put together. Unlike the individual who can be broken when alone, as a collective we are able to stand strong and can choose what we want the future to hold for our children. If enough of us stand together, use the 9-PAC Integrity Approach Model and language, and help guide and empower children through conscientious role modelling, my hope is that it will create a more peaceful, accepting, loving, kind and compassionate world.

One reason I wrote this book is because, as a life coach, I have discovered that many adults have issues that stem from their childhood. These issues stopped them from moving forward and becoming the person that they wanted to become. I have spoken earlier in the book about famous people who were told that they would amount to nothing. These negative words stick in the subconscious mind of the child, and affects their inner script as they grow into an adult. Many people lack the self-confidence to show their true self to the world, because of the criticism they received from an adult, who they saw as a role model in their life. They fear being the target of other's criticism yet again, so they hide, to avoid the pain and suffering they felt as a child.

The words our role models spoke to us as children were taken into our inner script because we were young and looked up to the people who said those words. These role models may have degraded us and said we were stupid, an idiot, useless or even gave us the impression, that because we were of a certain gender, had a sexual preference that differed from their belief system or were of a certain race or colour, that we were less important. You may also have had role models who said you were kind, you were intelligent, that you were capable of doing whatever you wanted to do in life and they showed you that they believed in your ability, to do whatever you chose to do. Both sets of role models shaped your inner script and this affected your thoughts, characteristics, beliefs, actions and how you now role model traits to the children you parent, guide or teach.

It is said that we all need to hear a positive phrase or event ten times more often than when we hear a negative phrase or event. Our brains are wired to hear the negative over positive, because in hunter–gather societies, negative things were life threatening and needed to be put directly into our subconscious script, so that we would remember them immediately. That is why it is so important for role models to unite, use a common empowering language and overlying belief on how to guide children. To ensure that our children hear the positive aspects of their character, so that they can see the gifts they have within themselves, and learn to enhance them and make them shine!

Virtues and Consciousness

Knowing about virtues and practicing them, are two different things. Many people know that virtues exist, but do not know how to best to use them, to enhance their inner script. Science and spirituality now believe that our thoughts and beliefs become our reality and that while we all have an individual consciousness, we also contribute to the wider social consciousness, within the world.

When an individual focuses on creating a lifelong habit of participating in a global virtue of the week (EthicalFoundations. com.au), or they select a personal virtue each morning, it helps them to reflect on what they would do differently in situations that did not turn out the way they hoped for. It also helps an individual to become aware of what characteristics they displayed when interacting with others and if they felt they could have displayed better virtues and behaviours, or if they want to enhance the characteristics that they employed. The amount of consciousness a role model shows the children they parent or guide, helps the children to also become more conscious. The role model uses exercises and stories to create an awareness of their own inner script, virtues and characteristics. Our mindset becomes more positive and confident as a person recognises and acknowledges themselves. This happens when the individual becomes more conscious of how their thoughts and behaviours affect others, their family, community and society. By reflecting on their virtues and by consciously choosing virtues to embody in their life, people raise their consciousness and become more objective, open-minded, tolerant, compassionate and peaceful in their lives.

When we act unconsciously, it becomes confusing when our interactions with others do not turn out the way we hoped for or our decisions have consequences that we do not like. We don't understand why things happened the way they did, because we are not aware of the character traits, virtues and beliefs that form our inner script and influence our reactions. When we do not understand what is running in our inner script, life becomes like a guessing game of how to act and communicate, and we never know what to do to get it right. This is very frustrating for adults and doubly frustrating for children, who often do not wish to hurt their schoolmates and friends with their words or behaviour.

A role model teaches about virtues through their communication with children and assists them in understanding how self-awareness is created and enhanced. By reflecting on how virtues can change and enhance their inner script, so they know why they are communicating and behaving the way they do. Also how it can help them to have the interactions and positive outcomes, they want. Every choice adults or children make has consequences and these consequences shape our world. Individuals need to make self-aware choices that will impact our future in a more positive way, so that our future societies can become the peaceful and considerate arenas that we want to live in. When children have the self-awareness and the self-confidence of knowing who they are, an inner strength is built and continues to strengthen with each aware interaction that they have. This is because as an aware individual they can continually evolve their inner script to become a more compassionate and loving person, each and every time they make contact with another individual.

When an individual reflects on their behaviour, they reflect on what feels right for them and they reflect on how it will affect others around them. Individuals should not rely on someone to simply telling them what to do or how to react, because that role model is working from their own script, which may or may not resonate with the child's inner script. A child who is told what to do does not truly understand the consequences of a decision they were instructed to take and they miss the valuable learning opportunities, of thinking through and discussing the options available to them and the potential consequences that can be generated from their decisions. A 9-PAC Integrity Approach role model guides and empowers the child by discussing what virtues could be used to help them decide which choices make the best sense for them and others. Enabling them to use their own innate skills and creative strategies to find win–win solutions that feel right for them. When guided to use these types of decision-making strategies, children feel more capable of handling whatever situation may arise, just like their adult role models do.

The importance of strengthening a child's inner virtues, becomes very important as they hit their preteen to teenage years, when they face different choices, such as smoking, drugs, alcohol and sex, which can be potential harmful to them. If a child partakes in any of these practices at a young age, it is because of feeling they need to fit in, prove themselves or because they want others to think they are tough. Because of these unaware choices that they made as young adults or teenagers they are likely to have inner script issues when they are older. However, we serve our children by developing and strengthening their inner script, so that we create ethical foundations within them and they will be better equipped to deal and respond to peer pressure at an older age. The sooner we commence serving a child in this capacity, the better, because children are facing these issues at younger and younger ages.

A person's vision of what life holds for them and their ability to live the life of their dreams, increases as they consciously make choices that stretch them beyond their comfort level. This helps them to continually evolve their inner script and become a better person each and every day. For example, a person might feel they are quite courageous in many aspects of their life, but they may feel scared to fly on an airplane, because of an event that happened during their childhood, by which they connect planes with death. The virtues of acceptance, courage, wisdom and reflection, could be called upon to help them to overcome this fear and be able to travel on an airplane for personal or business reasons. Acceptance would entail exploring where the fear came from and wisdom would allow the person to know that this fear may be detrimental to them reaching their dreams and it may allow them to overcome it step by step, as they make choices that are not driven by fear. Reflections would allow them to notice when their emotions, feelings and thoughts, were being influenced by their fear, and courage would help them to do whatever it takes, to overcome that fear in their mind and facing the fear, by flying to their event.

I once saw a clip showing a small boy attempting to jump over a barrier that was taller than him. He attempted this feat four times and his peers were all sitting by, watching him. The children on one side and adults the other. Not a single person gave any indication of disappointment or disapproval. After four attempts, all the children who were watching him, stood up and ran to him, surrounding him in a circle, like they do in football tackles, they cheered for him and ran back to their original spots. The child then ran towards the barrier and cleared it with ease. This is an example that illustrates that when others believe in you, you also start to believe in yourself. As your energy lifts and you feel empowered to achieve whatever you set your mind to. Imagine if children were as supportive of each other, as these children were in the example. Imagine in all role models supported children in this way? What would our world look like and what could we achieve if this type of support was normal in our society?

The Effect of Awareness and Awakening

In our society at the present moment, we have events of concern, where the safety of our teachers is in jeopardy in certain parts of the world and they need to learn combat skills in order to protect themselves, as some children become more aggressive towards them, not just verbally but physically. We must start to make the changes necessary to turn this trend around, so that we do not have to worry about our children or teachers being bullied when they are in school, or worse that they begin to behave in a bullying manner towards others and this behaviour becomes embodied throughout their entire life. How far will this behaviour get them? How happy do we think they would be to be continually hurting others? What sort of relationships – personal and professional – do you think they will they have? And how will their behaviour affect our society now and in the future?

How would these events be different if these children who bullied others would have been taught about virtues on a regular basis as younger children? Would they have learned to reflect on if their behaviour was patient, compassionate, considerate or gentle? How would these events change if the children were awakened and aware of how their actions affect others and society? Three ways to help children to become more aware is to teach them meditation, yoga and help them practice a one minute reflection, on a specific virtue each day. When individuals practice the above activities, they begin to feel that they are living true to their innate personality and that they are much more able to behave in a way that makes them feel good about themselves. They realise they are in control of the small everyday choices, such as how to think about other people, how to engage in positive self-talk and how to make choices, which lead to consequences that are empowering for the people they interact with and society.

To make these types of judgements a certain amount of discernment and detachment is required. Thoughts come into our mind, and can help to guide us towards the path of discernment. Where we can view other people's actions, communication and the issues they face, with a sense of detachment in order to make wise choices for ourselves and others. Discernment and detachment can also greatly reduce the anxiety and stress that we may feel, because of what others say or do. We can begin to see that the person's actions have nothing to do with us and everything to do with the other person's script and their need to control people and events, in order to get their own way.

How to Become Aware and Awakened

Consciousness operates on three distinct levels, and at each level an individual or child can become awakened and aware of their own inner script and how their thoughts, beliefs, self-talk, actions and emotions, affect others and the world around them. We will look at how individuals can become awakened at each level and how they can role model their own awareness to children, to help the children become awake and aware as well.

Individual Consciousness

When we are aware of our virtues and character traits, we choose how to interact with others. This brings a sense of peacefulness and contentment, because we are adhering to our own standards of what we believe is right and wrong. Life feels good when there is a sense of flow, we are conscience and confident in our virtues and we are being true to our authentic self.

Becoming aware and awakened at an individual level is actually quite a simple concept, but it is the consistency of doing these activities that we will present daily that makes the difference and allows people to become reflective masters, of their own inner script. When a person or child does anything that brings them joy and gratitude, such as daily walks around their neighbourhood, visiting with a friend at lunch, sitting in the sun reading a book or engaging in their favourite activity, happy thoughts are created and the person begins to feel a deep sense of gratitude. This helps them to create more experiences and thoughts of gratitude and joy, which become a habit and most people are aware that when something becomes a habit, it is ingrained into the subconscious and the person begins to think, act and communicate in a way that shows these virtues. These are some ways to become aware at an individual level, to focus on joy and keep yourself in a positive mindset.

As we discussed earlier in the chapter, another way for an individual or child to become aware of their inner script and make conscious choices on how they wish to interact with others is to practice a virtue daily or weekly and to reflect on how they are displaying this virtue and to notice how it impacts others around them and importantly, within themselves. Individuals can also reflect on how other people display this specific virtue and how it makes the individual feel, when they see it being role modelled in society or consequently not role modelled in society. It is a great exercise for parents or teachers to do with the children that they guide.

The last way I will discuss on how to become aware is through keeping a gratitude journal and writing down your expressions of gratitude on a daily basis. This will bring about a sense of awareness and of feeling of being more present in your life as you reflect on your day and what good things happened to you. This is a wonderful exercise you can use to help children learn gratitude and it will serve them well over their lifetime. Children will enjoy having their own little journal that they can write or draw their gratitude thoughts in. If you make time to write in your own journal, when they write in theirs, it can turn into a family bonding experience. Families can all say what they are grateful for at dinner time and parents can also put up a white board where the family can write what they are grateful for during the day. By creating a habit of gratitude or an attitude of gratitude, children continually focus on the positive. As discussed throughout this book, a positive mindset creates a positive inner script, which creates a more positive life. When there are many people cultivating attitudes of gratitude throughout the world, we will change the very fabric of our individual and societal consciousness. This leads us into how to become awakened through group consciousness.

Group Consciousness

There is a group consciousness, in which is a unity of thought regarding the common interest within that group. We discussed this when we learned about how cultural identity is created. Different group consciousnesses are created in social gatherings, between friends or people who have a common interest, such as people who do certain activities, like photography, dancing, yoga, bushwalking or football. Group consciousness does not just exist within a local group of people who meet weekly, it can exist among people all over the globe who participate in these activities. For example, people who follow a specific football team, will often have similar beliefs, thoughts and opinions about their team, and if you asked two people who were fans but lived on opposite sides of the globe, they could probably tell you a similar story about how people who are fans, think and behave in regard to that area of their life.

Group consciousness is created when a group of people with common beliefs, ideas and behaviours come together. Sometimes they are written down in a charter – girl guides or boy scouts, and everyone who belongs to the group must agree to these beliefs and ideas. However, some group consciousnesses are less professional and just exist because people often have similar personality traits and tend to believe the same things. An example of this would be photographers. If you travelled around the world and interviewed many people who did photography, you may find a type of loosely formed group consciousness. They may believe similar things about the profession, have similar likes and dislikes and interact with their clients in similar ways. There are jokes about certain type of professions, such as engineers or accountants, for acting in similar ways, even though, they may come from very different backgrounds.

To become aware of a group consciousness that you are part of, it is important to reflect on the combined thoughts, ideas, opinions, perceptions, beliefs and actions that the group shares. An individual can then decide if they wish to conform to their shared traits or be part of them, if the traits of the group help to enhance their own traits and if they approve of how the group treats others. A teacher or parent could ask their class or child to think about the group consciousness of a team they are part of such as a sports team or gymnastics team. The role model can ask the children to list the shared beliefs, thoughts, opinions and actions, that they believe the group holds and get them to compare them to their own inner script, to see if these two different consciousnesses work in a complimentary way or clash with their own beliefs. The role model can ask the children to see who may be leading the group consciousness, it might be the coach or a strong team player and to see if there is a formal list of expected thoughts and behaviours or is it much more loosely created. This exercise will help children to become aware of the group consciousness of any group they are in, even their family unit and to see how their inner script works with the group consciousness or against it. The child can decide if they want to be part of this consciousness or if they wish to no longer participate in it. They can also decide to enhance their virtues, or shift their own inner virtues to help enhance the group consciousness or to help to implement new virtues, that the group may decide are worthwhile ideas and adopt them.

Global Consciousness

Global consciousness is an understanding, that if many people focus on the same issue, such as a virtue of the week like friendliness, that this will influence the world at large, due to worldwide sense of unity on a certain virtue or idea.

Some people believe that when mass meditations have taken place, crime rates have dropped, and continued to remain low for the next few days after the meditations took place by spiritual groups collectively gathering – whether it be a coincidence or results of the gather who knows. It stands to reason that if the majority of people in the world were being mindful of a particular 'virtue of the week' such as kindness that there would be more people behaving with kindness towards one another.

In a smaller group collective consciousness – which always requires action to some degree – proved that a train could be moved when people collectively gathered to tilt a train from a track to save somebody who slipped between the platform and the train. On an individual basis it's a matter of if you think you can or you can't – you are right. You decide.

Global consciousness is created from individual and group consciousness. A country may have a group consciousness that helps people from that country define who they are and it creates a cultural identity that people who live in that country adhere to and believe in. But as stated earlier, you cannot control other people's thoughts, beliefs and actions like, some countries attempt to. Some individuals have such inner conviction, strength and integrity, that they stand up to their government, by not conforming to their wishes and consequently are punished and mistreated by those in power. This is where all individuals living as awakened beings, can help others in their plight, by doing what we can to stand as one, on a global level.

These large group consciousnesses helps to form the global consciousness of the world. A person can understand global consciousness in terms of what humanity thinks or what traits many humans believe are positive character traits to have, regardless of their religion, cultural identity or group identity. Now if you go to different parts of the world, the global consciousness may look a bit different to different people, because their group consciousness affects the way they see the global consciousness.

The 9-PAC Integrity Approach Model, aims to create a global consciousness of how role models communicate and guide the children they parent or work with. As we have talked about earlier in the book, an individual can make massive impacts in the world. By writing a book, making a movie or documentary, creating a movement, an invention or discovering a cure that people all over the world resonate with and begin to adapt into their inner script. By role modelling these new traits daily to the children in your life you will create a ripple that causes others to adopt these beliefs and the individual consciousness now becomes a group consciousness that can become a global consciousness, if enough people decide to role model consistently in their lives. One person really can become the change they want to see in the world.

A 9-PAC role model can help children to understand global consciousness, by asking their children or their class to look at what virtues they think make up our global consciousness right now. The role model can ask them to think at the group consciousness level and the national consciousness level and see what they think all these groups believe in and approve of. They could look at the United Nations Charter of Rights and Freedoms and see if they believe these traits are the traits that our global consciousness follows. The children could look at how these traits are different and begin to reflect on why they might be different. They could draw up their own United Nations Charter and see what virtues they would like to see shared on a global consciousness level. The class could then look at how their own individual consciousness and the group consciousnesses that they are part of, could shift their traits and practice new virtues, in order to create a new global consciousness that would be better for our society, the earth and all things that live on it. They could see how they can personally change their inner script to help model these traits they want to see in the world, to others around them. This type of awareness truly helps children and their role models understand that change really does happen at an individual level and that massive global change can happen, because one person decided to change their inner script and it spread out though the world and created change.

Many amazing people have created global consciousness change such as Nelson Mandela, Jane Goodall, Steve Jobs, Oprah Winfrey and many, many more. I believe that our job as 9-PAC Integrity Approach Role Models is to help children understand that they CAN be the change they want to see in the world. That helping them to awaken and become aware of all the consciousnesses they are a part of, can help them to be able to ultimately shift these consciousnesses into what they want them to become, so that our society and world functions in a more compassionate and objective way.

Awakening the power that lies within all of us, comes from our willingness to constantly examine our internal awareness and uncover and overcome the internal issues that may often lie hidden in our inner script. The power lies within discovering who you really are, what your inner script is and who you want to become. It hinges on taking the necessary steps, to discover new ways to evolve yourself and to cultivate more positive virtues, character traits, skills and positive behaviours.

Who We Interact with Affects our Consciousness

You may have heard people say that, "Who you hang around with, determines your character" or that "The five people you interact with the most, you are going to end up like." If we teach our children to be kind, they will become attracted to friends with similar values. If we teach our children that violence is acceptable, they will be comfortable around violent people and violent forms of entertainment. Global and group beliefs take time to change, but if we as role models focus on the virtues we would like to see in the world, we can start to shift these beliefs, simply by believing or not believing in them and when enough people possess a mentality that benefits the world and stop believing in a certain mentality that is detrimental to the world, it changes the global consciousness to what people are now focusing on and living.

If Role Models can teach children and those around them to keep an open mind, humanity can learn to objectively view different perspectives and issues from new angles that they had not yet considered and learn to listen to what everyone has to share. These new perspectives will touch on various truths and an authentic truth of love, compassion and tolerance will begin to reveal itself, until all parties involved come to a common agreement that these virtues are acceptable things to teach our children and model in our lives. If we all speak from our authentic truth, which contributes to being a part of the whole truth, we will create a new global consciousness that has all the positive virtues in it and our societies will change into the utopian societies that we believe are possible.

When we take time to reflect, it is the same as having a two-way conversation. We use self-discipline to remove all the noise in our head and objectively listen to what our inner self is telling us. The answers to all of our problems are within each of us and all we need to do is listen and follow our hearts. This is why it is so important to awaken and practice reflection, so that we are not running someone else's advice constantly through our head. It is also important to allow our children to share their views on issues and then offer a perspective they may not have considered before. This allow them to make their own decisions and we can support them regardless of what they choose.

Most people learn through the experience of doing something themselves. For example, you can learn to drive a car by actually getting behind the wheel and going for a drive, or you can seek advice on how to drive from an expert. Often people do not understand a concept completely until they have experienced it themselves. There is a massive gap between being told something and doing it yourself. Although you may have received mountains of information and spoken to many people, it still does not compare with experiencing it for yourself. Regardless of where we are at, there is always more to learn, which is why life is a journey. There will be times when your child, or other special people in your life, make choices that are detrimental to themselves and which impact on you and those around them.

For example, many people decide to take drugs and some become addicted until they can stand it no more. Relationships are affected and everyone involved can suffer the damaging effects until that person seeks help and decides to commit to their wellbeing. By purposefully using their self-discipline to do whatever it takes to resolve this overwhelming period in their life. Each person has an inner knowing of what they need to do, but they sometimes feel that life is too tough and that they do not have the potential that others see within them. They lack the self-belief that they are worthy of the love and support that they are so freely offered and given.

The suicide rate continues to grow amongst so many in our society who have enormous potential to help others yet do not, because they cannot see themselves as being useful to anyone. Depression can set in contributing to the growing mental health issues also. Many people feel they are unlovable and have some story going around in their head, either consciously or subconsciously, which was created by an experience they had at some stage, where they formed a preconceived notion that life is not meant to be like it is. Life is tough, and this is why it is important that we teach our children from the very beginning about kindness, compassion and acceptance. By teaching them these lessons we reduce the number of challenges they have to face, as well as how to deal with those challenges when they do arise.

Everyone has challenges in their life. Our personalities and characteristics are unique to us and once we overcome them we can see them as gifts that can strengthen our character. There is always light at the end of the tunnel, it is just so dark that sometimes we forget what light looks like. Faith, trust, courage and self-discipline are called upon more frequently during difficult times and the day will come when the tip of the mountain has been reached and things get easier and the constant uphill struggle has been achieved. It takes self-discipline to live in the present moment and tackle issues head on, rather than living in the future moments of what you wish life was like. Putting first steps first is important.

To role model inner knowing to a child, we can reflect and share what insights we gained during the course of our reflection or meditation, what we felt instinctively and took action on; as well as, how it made us feel. For example, if kindness was the virtue of the week and we were out shopping and the person in the queue in front of us was short $10, and did not have any other way of paying their bill, we could offer to lend them or just give them the $10. This action would not only make them feel good, but it would make us feel good as well. I recall doing this once at a shopping centre and the person expressed their gratitude and told me that I had restored their faith in humanity. I recall thinking "Wow, and that only cost me $10?" In actual fact, it did not even cost me the $10 as they insisted on repaying the money so I told them that a family member had a shop nearby, and the person returned the money, via the family member, next time they were in town. I suspect they made a special trip as they had mentioned they lived some distance out of town. There are times in our life when we need to reflect on what to do and times in our life when we act impulsively. Learn to trust your instincts, because they are often right. A little kindness is never wasted and can go a long, long way.

The sooner we equip our children with tools and strategies that enable them to become self-assured, humble, confident, socially and morally responsible human beings. The sooner this world transforms and we treat each other and the earth the way we all deserve to be treated, with kindness, acceptance, compassion and respect, the better. It has been said that a journey of a thousand steps begins with a single step, so therefore, by letting your own light shine, you will allow others to shine too, until the earth is glowing as brightly as the sun.

Present Moment

Living in the present moment removes stress and anxiety from our lives as when we focus on either the past or the future we find we are often anxious, worried or stressed out something that is not happening right now. We waste a lot of time unnecessarily.

Living in the present moment allows us to experience and truly take in whatever we are experiencing at that precise moment, the joy of being with family and friends, our surroundings, the noises we hear, the sights before us – just being, breathing and being right there, then, and now. Take it all in.

When we are experiencing a present moment, we are consciously aware of what is taking place at that point in time. When we are with friends, we are truly present and listen to what is being said and quickly recognise when we are wanting to say something in return, or that we were about to interrupt them or worse still have interrupted them already, before the other person has finished speaking. We learn to pull ourselves into line, because our awareness about our thoughts has grown, and we are aware that we slipped into the future, because we stopped listening to what they are presently saying and have already thought of our response.

When we truly listen, we allow people to finish saying what they feel they need to say and then take a moment to think about our response before consciously opening our mouth. Next time you are at a coffee shop or out for lunch and the waiter or waitress takes an order for a group and returns with a long black coffee and asks the group who ordered the long black, there will be at least one person who puts their hand up and states what they ordered, which wasn't the answer to the question. This is not what the waiter or waitress asked. The person who responded by informing them of what they ordered is attempting to be helpful, but the minute they raise their hand or open their mouth, the waitress may start heading to the person who puts their hand up, even though they are not the person that ordered the long black coffee. The person who responded was not living in the present moment, and had jumped to the future because they did not hear what was being asked or attempted to be helpful but were not. It would have been helpful to answer the question or ask the question again if others did not hear in the first place. Watch what happens next time you go out with friends.

There are many times when we attempt to be helpful but hinder the process, because we did not truly listen to what was being asked in the first place. Being present helps all individuals involved, because when someone is providing a service to us and asking the necessary questions, we can help them achieve their purpose by cooperating and listening to the question. Being present when talking to a child about important issues, such as what happened in their day and how they are dealing with both positive and negative experiences teaches them we are truly listening and builds a relationship of trust where they feel they can count on us if they ever need us. Being present in times of meditation and reflection, means that we recognise when our mind is busy and we take the time required to clear our mind, so that once the clutter in our head disperses, we clearly feel, know or see, what action we need to take.

We can role model the present moment by participating in a round-table discussion with children at the dinner table, or in a group setting. We can share part of ourselves and our experiences as well, so that they can see that regardless of our position, authority, age, or gender, we are all growing spiritual beings. Children need to learn that life is full of ups and downs and that we call upon our inner strength as required in times of difficulty. We all have friends that move away, which may make us sad, new experiences can be frightening and moments in our life, where we can be helpful, kind or when others rely on us to do something. It is discussing the everyday moments that provides small opportunities for awareness to grow and children have the ability to quickly see how one small action multiplied, can have an effect on the whole class, school, community or world. Children have much more insight than we sometimes give them credit for.

Internal Power

It is crucial to have an awareness of our inner strength and that we all have numerous virtues within us that we can bring to the surface anytime we choose. By frequently focusing on virtues either daily or weekly, a child will soon realise that in order to practice one virtue, they are all interrelated, and although one virtue might be the focus, it is impossible to practice it on its own. Practicing a virtue once a month or school term, is not as effective as the link between action, awareness and conscious living is. For example, if the virtue of the week was helpfulness and a child saw another child accidentally drop an object on the floor and picked it up for them, that would also be a kind thing to do. Other virtues such as cooperation, consideration, thoughtfulness and service, may also come into play when the child helped the other child. They are all positive attributes, viewed through a different lens. Once a school term or month, does provide sufficient time for constant growth and reflection, so that is why I recommend doing a daily or weekly practice of reflecting on virtues. Balance and moderation are required yet again.

Teaching and learning go hand in hand as nobody escapes life without learning the lessons that it strives to teach each and every one of us. Do you ever notice that if you do not learn a life lesson that you keep getting the same lesson over and over until you learn it? It just comes in different ways and can start as a whisper and if not learned each time it becomes more obvious until it feels like you've been hit by a Mack truck. Assisting children to increase their awareness and to recognise and acknowledge what they have in life and what others may not have, is an opportunity to practice appreciation and gratitude. Usually, children sincerely want to create equality, as they are compassionate, kind and caring and have pure intentions due to their age. It is important that their role models continue to encourage this, as well as discuss virtues such as wisdom, justice, idealism and generosity. It is also important to teach our children about the wisdom of setting limits by using their discretion and inner knowing so that they are not taken advantage of or place trust in people who may not be trustworthy at this stage in their life.

As previously mentioned balance and moderation in everything is extremely important. Children want to share what they have so readily and there are things that can be shared and given away, and things that require discussion with parents or other role models first.

The future generation can be powerful beyond belief if given the opportunity to go forth and transform the world by looking within and discovering their own true potential and serving the world in a way that brings joy to themselves and others. Not everyone needs, or wants, to be someone famous or rich but everyone needs and wants to live a happy, peaceful, contented life where they feel fulfilled. Anyone and everyone can do that and to do that it is very simple and basic. Treat people how you would like to be treated, especially yourself.

CHAPTER 8 – SUMMARY:

- When your subconscious and conscious are united you feel in harmony with the world and that the universe is supporting you

- When you feel you are living as intended your energy levels increase

- Vibration levels surround us all and we attract what we put out into the world, this changes as we change internally

- You are more powerful than you realise, you control your mind, it does not control you

- Taking the time to share with children benefits you in the long term – as well as them

- Educating future generations about self-awareness is the best gift we can give to the progress of humanity

CHAPTER 9

Community

Definition

- A group of people who live in the same area (such as a city, town or neighbourhood)

- A group of people who have the same interests, religion, race, etc.

- A group of nations

"Small acts
when multiplied
by millions of people
can transform the world."

Howard Zinn

It's Not My Job

This is a story about four people named Everybody, Somebody, Anybody and Nobody.

There was an important job to be done and Everybody was asked to do it. Everybody was sure Somebody would do it. Anybody could have done it, but Nobody did it. Somebody got angry about that, because it was Everybody's job. Everybody thought Anybody could do it but Nobody realised that Everybody wouldn't do it. It ended up that Everybody blamed Somebody when Nobody did what Anybody could have done.

Wouldn't it be great if we could? What a different world we would live in. We'd all be living our dream life and have a dream job which felt like we were living our purpose and not getting up and heading off to work so we could just exist and, for some, have the lifestyle we desire.

There is unity in the word community. It is meant to be there. It is a sign from the universe that we need to come together and be united, in order to create the vision that we all want to see in this world. Deep down I believe that every one of us wants to live a joyful, happy and peaceful life. I have seen that the path that will lead us all there is one in which we become self-aware in every possible way, so that we can choose appropriate actions and consequences; that will help us advance on our journey. Not a single one of us can survive and fulfil this dream without supporting, encouraging and empowering each other. But we can only do this by mastering ourselves first.

The 9-PAC Integrity Approach Model is a system that parents, childcare educators and teachers, can employ when communicating and guiding children. It is a system that encourages role models to listen attentively to the children, be mindful of them and help them to cultivate courage, confidence and positive self-talk. While also creating an empowering and supportive community, at home, at a childcare centre or in a classroom, where they can learn and grow. In this chapter, we will discuss what I believe our community and society will look like when children have been raised to live mindfully. Are self-aware and feel self-confident in their own abilities, so that they joyfully contribute to their families, communities and society.

The majority of role models, specifically parents, childcare educators and teachers, realise what an important and powerful role they hold in our society, helping to shape our future leaders, teachers and policy makers. The 9-PAC Integrity Approach Model was created in order to lay the foundation for a role model group consciousness built with the virtues of trust, compassion, tolerance, kindness, awareness, responsibility, confidence, self-awareness, empowerment, reflection, objectivity and assertiveness. It is a group consciousness that invites adults to use a common, empowering language, an objective decision making system and employs reflective exercises, to help children learn about their inner scripts. Including how to enhance their characteristics or shift them so that they can become change makers in our world. It is a model that helps children to understand how their decisions and consequences will affect others and empowers them to create win–win solutions, for everyday problems that they encounter. As well as for global issues that need to be solved in our world. The 9-PAC Approach helps role models teach children to view others differences with wonder and curiosity. To hear what others are proposing so that they can learn from other people who have different scripts from their own. It encourages both the role models and children to continue to awaken and become more self-aware as they move forward on their life journey. It also teaches them to never stop refining and enhancing their innate skills and talents, which make them uniquely suited to serve our society in different ways.

Our governments provide a curriculum for all childcare educators, teachers and home school parents to follow, which can be overwhelming and restrictive. But the 9-PAC Integrity Approach Model is filled with tools and exercises, to help role models fulfil their duty to our future citizens, while still teaching the required curriculum. It helps role models to teach the foundations of integrity, with case study and creative exercises, that encourage learning within a supportive environment, where teachers and students all learn from each other, in a harmonious community atmosphere.

Through the 9-PAC Integrity Approach Model, parents, childcare educators and teachers, collectively interact with children in a way that builds their self-confidence and self-awareness on a continual basis, not only at home, but in their communities and classrooms also. Imagine how quickly a child would become self-aware and self-assured of their own abilities, if they were in constant contact with role models who modelled the 9-PAC Integrity Approach, at every point in their day. There is an old African proverb that says, "It takes a community to raise a child," and that logic is the reason that I wrote this book, in order to help parents, childcare educators and teachers, who are so essential in the development of a child life.

The 9-PAC Integrity Approach Model helps role models to create consistency, stability, security and a constant supportive environment, where a child feels safe, loved, respected and accepted, which create an emotional stable inner script. Unfortunately, not all the adults in a child's life, will be 9-PAC role models, so I believe that it is vitally important, that children get to interact with as many positive and supportive role models as possible, within their families, care centres and schools. These role models can create a consistently supportive community atmosphere that is filled with empowering language, so that children will have the ability to learn positive systems and self-awareness, from more than just one adult in their lives. The more positivity that children are around and hear, the more they are able to cultivate positive self-talk and work from a positive inner script.

Celebrating Our Differences

When we educate our children at a young age that everyone they meet has different inner scripts, cultural identities, unique talents and virtues, children open their minds and hearts to understand how those differences can be helpful. When they are in a group situation or working on a group project, their awareness of those different skills and virtues can help to create imaginative solutions and win–win opportunities. Children also learn to actively acknowledge and celebrate the other person's unique virtues and talents, rather than judge them, against their own cultural 'norms'. Teaching our children tolerance at a young age helps them to cultivate the virtues of friendliness, respect, kindness, compassion and peacefulness.

When we teach our children to employ these positive character qualities, when they interact with other children, they establish a community environment that promotes cooperation, communicate and collaboration. These virtues will promote the advancement of our civilisation, because children become accustomed to living in a supportive community when children view this way of living as a normal way of life, and they work to create this type of community atmosphere in our society on a family, group and global level.

Everyone's purpose in life is different, but powerful. Whatever each person's purpose is, it will bring them peace and joy if they are allowed to authentically create the life their skills and abilities have prepared them to live. By doing what they love and feel joyful doing so, we are supporting children to discover all of their talents. When we can allow children to follow their heart and trust their instincts, make mistakes and learn from them, and always have a supportive role model to help guide them, they will become creative and confident in the pursuit of following their dreams; which will serve society in useful and creative ways.

Parents, childcare educators and teachers can acknowledge the gifts our future adults possess and help them to become aware of, enhance and reflective on how these skills and talents can help themselves and others in life. This would create a world of individuals who serve our world in confident and ethical ways, which would help to create a beautiful, peaceful, united and caring, global community.

Children are very accepting of what others say about them and tend to believe what is said to them, whether it is truth or not. 9-PAC Integrity Approach Role models can become children's guiding lights by educating them, loving them and supporting them to become the best people they can be; not only during their childhood years, but helping to mentor them in all phases of their life. Just like building a house, or any major construction project, the stronger the foundation, the stronger a child's inner script will be; to handle the challenges that will come their way. We hope that all children will have the 9-PAC Integrity Approach Model tools and strategies modelled to them, so they will know how to effectively handle the tests and difficulties they face with integrity and be able to make aware and contentious decisions, that take other's feelings, needs and wants into account. Role modelling is a service that parents, teachers and childcare educators provide to our children, families, communities and to society, as we are responsible for building our future generations inner script, affecting not only their lives as they grow up, but our lives, their children's lives and their grandchildren's lives as well.

Service Brings Joy

Serving others can bring immense joy and happiness to each of us, as it allows us to guide children bring out the best in themselves, spiritually, emotionally, intellectually and physically. It is rare to meet a role model who was not joyful and grateful, to be able to help a student or child achieve wonderful things in their life. 9-PAC Integrity Approach role models affect children's behaviour in positive ways, by helping them to have the most aware and positive inner script that is possible for each child, at each moment in their lives. Not all children will become as aware as others are, and that is okay. If role models are able to provide learning opportunities for each child and assist them to build habits of self-reflection, tolerance and observation, in a supportive community environment, it will help the child on their life path and lead any child to make better decisions in their life, which affect all of us in society, in a more positive way.

For example, to use a 'tree-like' metaphor, children are like trees. Trees need air, water, sunlight, space and nutrients to grow. All of these things are provided by the earth or their human caregivers. Every growing thing requires some sort of nurturing to thrive and reach its full potential. Humans, regardless of age, need the same nurturing to help them grow into the individuals they are born to be. This nurturing concept, created the very fabric of the 9-PAC Integrity Approach Model. Just like a forest of trees helps each other grow, to create a community of health and prosperity. When children learn how to work together in a positive and supportive community, they too can achieve more together, than they could independently.

Nothing is as powerful as a unified community and if all role models in a child's life worked together, using a common supportive language and tools which helped to empower our children, our world would have an amazing future where every child grew up feeling loved, accepted and appreciated. This would make a massive difference in each child's life and propel them to a greatness that we cannot even dream of. Everyone needs just one person to be their rock, and as a 9-PAC role model, you have that opportunity with every child you meet or interact with. As a role model, you influence a child's inner script, which helps to create the person they will become. As they grow up, these children become members of the wider community and in turn, influence the children and other adults around them.

The more people that want to leave the world in a better place than they found it and want to contribute to raising children with integrity, the more we are able to change the world and contribute to a positive shift in global collective consciousness. But this takes a community of people, who all believe in the same ideals, beliefs and methods, to raise children with integrity, which helps them to become the best individual they can be. I believe that the 9-PAC Integrity Approach Model can be the foundation of this new mindset shift, which teaches individuals how to mentor children in positive and encouraging ways.

United Community

There is an energy that can be felt when a person is in a community of like-minded people. This living flow has an inner strength that people gravitate toward and can throw their support behind, as it resonates with their virtues and their inner script. It becomes a force of change and people are attracted to the intention behind the energy. The 9-PAC Integrity Approach Model can become a living community mindset and model that role models from all over the world can feel good about using and implementing in their lives.

Using this model in order to help their children or the children they teach, grow and evolve into amazing human beings.

I hope the ideas, concepts, strategies and exercises in this book have resonated with you deeply and you feel the energy of change and empowerment that can be enhanced and carried forward in your own life. This energy can help you become a role model that a child in your community needs to help them grow and expand into an aware and reflective human being, who can make discerning choices that will affect our communities and societies in diverse and positive ways.

When role models put this intention first in their life, they can evolve themselves to become better people. By refining their inner script, healing their wounds and becoming aware of patterns and beliefs that are detrimental to them, so that they can become the very best role model that they can be. Children deserve the very best role models we can provide for them. How compassionate and tolerate our society is depends on how positive, peaceful and objective these children's beliefs and behaviours are as they move into positions of power, in their adult lives. How well our schools, communities, businesses and governments function, will come as a direct result of the decisions future adults make. These future adults are the children who you are role modelling for, right now. Therefore, it is vitally important that we as role models, decide to do something about our future society, today.

It is empowering to know that each one of us can make a difference in the life of a child, which will eventually affect each and every one of us in ways we cannot yet comprehend. If we create a community consciousness of empowerment, respect, support, compassion, tolerance, kindness, awareness and discernment in our own communities now, we can immediately affect the lives of the children around us in profound ways. This community consciousness can spread to become a worldwide movement, as people also feel drawn to the resonance of the concepts laid out in this book. Everyone can learn how to become better role models; who can begin to Raise Children with Integrity, right now! There is no time to lose, as we know children grow up so fast and they form their inner script early on in childhood.

We can help our older children and adult children learn how to not only become better role models, but to become better human beings. Who recognise that the choice they are making right now affect the children around them, our communities and our global society. We can serve the world by helping to role model the 9-PAC Integrity Approach Model in our own lives, starting today. We can begin to become aware and reflective of our own inner script and how we can evolve it daily, with reflection of virtues, active listening, role modelling aware decision making and speaking in empowering language, to people and children around us. I believe it is our sincere duty as heart-centred adults, to become a 'being' who makes whatever changes we can right now in the world, to authentically become the change that we want to see in our families, communities and society.

I would like to leave you with a list of reflective questions that I hope will empower you to start on your inner reflective journey today and begin to actively serve our children, by becoming the best role model you can.

- Do you judge others based on their physical attributes and differences?

- Do you see other people's unique skills and talents?

- Do you help to celebrate and support other people's skills and talents?

- How would you describe your character and personality?

- How would others describe your character and personality?

- Do you know what virtues you want to display in your character?

- Are you aware of who created your inner script and what patterns, beliefs, opinions and perceptions you are running, and are they authentically yours?

- Do you speak with an empowering language to yourself and the children around you?

- Is your self-talk positive or negative?

- Do you actively listen to what children say to you and digest it before you respond?

- Do you offer children appropriate decisions to choose from and then support children's decisions, even if you don't agree with them?

- Can you humbly accept the consequences of your decisions and admit when you make mistakes and learn from them?

- What is your decision-making style and do you seek to control your inner script or control others?

- Do you have control over your thoughts, beliefs and actions?

- Are you in control of your inner script and what patterns you run?

- Are you aware of what your individual, family and group cultural identity traits, beliefs and behaviours are and do you agree with them?

- How do these identities, affect your interactions with others and your tolerance and compassion?

- Are you aware of your individual and group consciousness traits, beliefs and behaviours and do you agree with those?

- Are you aware of your inner script and have worked to bring your subconscious beliefs and thoughts to your conscious mind, so that you can decide to enhance these traits and characteristics or shift them?

- How often do you reflect on virtues and gratitude and seek to become a more peaceful and compassionate person?

- Do you believe that it takes a community to raise and child and do you believe that you are doing your part to help the children in your community thrive and be able to evolve into their true potential?

- Are you a pillar of support and encouragement for the people around you and the children you guide?

- Do you create a supportive community atmosphere, for children to learn in?

- Are you teaching children to be true to themselves and use their gifts to serve their communities?

- Are you becoming the best role model you can be, in each moment?

- Do you radiate out integrity, confidence and kindness to the people around you and in your community?

- Do you believe that you can become the change this world needs, by helping to Raise Children with Integrity?

- Do you want to start right NOW?

Footnotes:

Chapter title definitions:

http://www.merriam-webster.com/dictionary

Claire Newton

(http://www.clairenewton.co.za/my-articles/the-five-communication-styles.html)

Trish Corbett

Author, Life Coach & Entrepreneur

Trish is an author, life coach and entrepreneur.

Her first job was as a typesetter in the art department of a local printing company. After that, she had various jobs as a typesetter and desktop publisher for a variety of companies and universities.

After many years, she decided that she had enough of those fields. That's when Trish moved on to become an office manager and ultimately a personal assistant for hospital executives.

Fortunately, the time she spent working at universities and hospitals allowed her to broaden her skills and further her education by taking several courses. Trish has also earned a Welfare Certificate and a Public Relations Certificate. Additionally, she is a qualified Myers Briggs Facilitator.

Inspired by her prior careers, Trish started her own company. Through Ethical Foundations, she works as a life coach and Virtues Project facilitator. She believes that both roles sync in a way that enables her to be an effective author and share her message to a wider audience.

Her volunteer activities include telephone counselling for Lifeline and coaching high school students as a Max Potential Coach.

Trish Corbett is the author of *How To Raise Children With Integrity* and lives in New South Wales, Australia.

Recommended
Resources

THE VIRTUES PROJECT™

The Virtues Project™ is a global grassroots initiative to inspire the practice of virtues in everyday life, sparking a global revolution of kindness, justice, and integrity in more than 100 countries.

Workshops are held throughout the world teaching The Five Strategies:

1. Speak The Language of the Virtues

2. Recognise Teachable Moments

3. Set Clear Boundaries

4. Honour the Spirit

5. Offer the Art of Spiritual Companioning™

Educator's Virtues Cards, character education cards for the classroom and more.

The Virtues Shop distributors of The Virtues Project™ materials:

Virtues Project Educator's Guide, simple ways to create a culture of character for schools, daycares, etc.

The Family Virtues Guide, parenting with virtues; tools for parents and children to cultivate virtues in the family.

The Virtues Project™ website to learn more about The Virtues Project™.

www.virtuesproject.com